Praise for Abuse OF Men BY Women: it happens, it hurts, and it's time to get real about it

"Ann Silvers' book, *Abuse OF Men BY Women*, addresses a much-neglected social problem. The book accurately reflects the latest social science research yet it is highly readable, the writing clear and lively.

Ann has done an outstanding job identifying the tactics used by abusive and controlling women, and how men find themselves entrapped in these relationships. She also offers practical solutions for women who are abusing, men who are abused, and their families. Great book! Well done!"

—John Hamel, LCSW, Author, *Gender-Inclusive Treatment of Intimate Partner Abuse, 2nd Edition: Evidence-based Approaches*, and Editor-in-Chief, *Partner Abuse*.

What do abused men who have read the book have to say about it? "Wow!"

"All I can say is Wow! I wish I had read this 20 years ago. This would have saved me hundreds of thousands of dollars and years of my life. This is something that my 18-year-old son will have to read. This is a gift to every 'son' out there. Thank you for the work you are doing. Men of all ages need to read this. I think the issue is much bigger than anyone even realizes."

"WOW! A great achievement here. The glass ceiling of prejudicial thinking may very well be broken with the publication of this very informative book. I see a piece of my life's experience on almost every page."

"Wow! It is a wonderful book and brilliantly insightful! I couldn't put it down. It draws upon personal experience and extensive research which brings about the urgency to explore the abuse of men by women. It is a powerful recommendation to counselors, social workers, lawyers, teachers, pastors, and all who are in a position to assist men and women dealing with this issue."

"This synthesis of the latest research in abuse of men by women is a major breakthrough, showing what is happening, giving clarity, offering a new awareness of an issue that is commonly ignored and disregarded: the abuse of men by women. It has the potential of becoming *the* instrument for measuring and defining partner abuse. Ann also offers solutions to relieve the suffering and devastation it causes."

"It's as if Ann had known me and my ex all our lives and was writing the book from an invisible observation point in the house. I recognized myself and others in the examples. I saw my paternal grandpa, my father-in-law, and many close friends. Ann's book will provide understanding, initiate healing, and give hope to many men out there. I wish I'd had a copy of the book when I first started dating and especially, before I divorced."

"The subject matter is rare, shocking, simply put and yet so refreshing. The book brings to the light of day an old problem that dates back centuries and that went unnoticed all this time."

Abuse OF men BY women

It happens, it hurts, and it's time to get real about it

Ann Silvers M.A.

SILVERSPUBLISHING

ISBN: 978-0-9834338-7-3

Printed in the United States of America
10 9 8 7 6 5 4 3 2 1

Published by Silvers Publishing, LLC
Gig Harbor, Washington, USA
www.silverspublishing.com

This book is dedicated to the man who looked at me with tears in his eyes and said, "You have to write the book," and all the other men and women who wanted their stories included in the hopes that individuals dealing with abuse of men by women in isolation may be helped and a light may be shone on the subject.

Contents—Overview

Contents—Detailed

xiv

This book is focused on partner abuse OF men BY women.

OF and BY are capitalized because when I first talked about the topic of women abusing men, "abuse of men" was often mistakenly heard as "abusive men." I realized that we are so conditioned to automatically think of men as abusers that I needed emphasis on the *of* and *by* in order to get people to slow down and grasp that I was talking about men being the target of the abuse, and women the source of the abuse, not the other way around.

A summary of this book can be found in the full-color booklet: *a quick look at Abuse OF men BY women*

A few of the abuse stories used in this book are taken out of the headlines, but for the most part, the stories are those of men I have met or talked to personally, or of abused men's partners, family members, or friends I have met or talked to personally.

I include identifying details and real names in the stories that have been previously outed by newspapers and other public sources. While I alter the others to protect identities, the stories are *not* exaggerated or intentionally distorted. Quotes from abused men and their family members, and women who abused a man, appear without names. (I forgo the made-up names often used in other self-help books.)

Abuse of men by women is an everyday occurrence. The examples are all around us. If we aren't seeing them, we aren't looking for them.

I understand partner abuse because I've witnessed it, studied it, and lived it.

I have a legacy of abuse on both sides of my family tree. On my mom's branch were three brothers, including my grandfather, who married three sisters. All three men were tyrants, abusing their children and wives. My father's family was the flip side of the same story. My paternal grandmother, Lavina, was an abusive mother and wife who outlived her quiet-spoken, beaten-down husband.

I know what it is like to be the target of abuse from a partner. I experienced financial, psychological, and emotional abuse by a boyfriend. It took me a long time to figure out what was going on. He was determined to destroy me. I became determined to not let that happen.

There are people who object to the subject of women abusing men being acknowledged because they worry that it somehow undermines women's rights. Let me assure you, I am not anti-female or anti-women's rights. I came of age with, and participated in, the women's movement. Long before I became interested in the topic of abuse of men by women, I spent a lot of time and energy studying partner abuse in relationships where women are the targets.

When I went back to school in my thirties to become a counselor, my college degrees included a Minor in Women's Studies. I have participated in many events promoting the advancement of women, including the United Nations Conference on Women in Beijing in 1995.

Until I witnessed a male friend being abused by his wife, I was among the hordes that don't appreciate the amount of abuse men are experiencing from their female partners or the devastation that it creates. My eyes were opened through that experience.

Once my eyes were opened, I saw how prevalent abuse of men by women is. I realized I had been missing it in some of my clients and I became much better at recognizing the signs that a woman was being abusive or a man was being abused.

Since I started talking about my interest in abuse of men by women, people have been coming out of the woodwork with their stories. Sometimes it's men who have been, or are currently being, abused by a wife, girlfriend, or ex. Sometimes it's family members who have suffered through watching their beloved brother, father, or son be manipulated and abused, or endured the loss of him from their lives as he attempts to please an unreasonable partner.

Even now, when I think I have become acclimatized to how widespread the problem is, I am sometimes still taken aback by the frequency at which I randomly bump into people who have been directly impacted by a woman abusing a man.

I have become keenly aware of the information vacuum that exists for, and about, men, women, and families in this situation. I am frustrated by partner abuse resources that give lip service to the existence of abuse of men by women but then provide only examples where "he" abuses and "she" is the target.

I hope this book will fill in the void, help all those directly impacted by abuse of men by women, and instigate a broader recognition and concern about the topic. Let's get the conversation started.

Part One

Setting the stage

Women abuse men? Does that happen?

Male targets of abuse by women
have a great deal of challenge
understanding the situation they find themselves in.
The phenomenon of abuse OF men BY women is very
widespread but largely ignored or discounted.

What are we talking about here?

A man separated from his wife finds a file box she left by the door to his rental home. He is devastated to discover that the contents reveal that they have several years of unpaid taxes she previously led him to believe were paid.

A woman's unchecked anxiety compels her to demand that her husband do things her way or deal with her anger.

A man is woken up in the middle of the night by his wife pounding him with the clock radio. She hits him in both arms, the chest, and face—right beside his eye—before he flees the house.

Lying, manipulation, misuse of funds, badgering, and physical attack are a few of the many ways women abuse their male partners.

> Abuse of men by women goes against cultural expectations for both genders.

The men who are the targets of this abuse can be shocked and bewildered by it. It goes against cultural expectations for both genders. Women are thought of as considerate and nurturing. Men are expected to be strong and in control.

Although women can and do abuse men in many situations, this book focuses on partner abuse of men by women in romantic relationships: dating, cohabitation, marriage, divorce, post-divorce, and post-breakup.

I am *not* saying women are abusive. I am saying that there are abusive women. I am *not* saying all women, or most women, abuse men. I am saying that sometimes they do, and it is important to talk about it.

Is abuse OF men BY women really a problem?

Yes! And a very common one.

Exactly how much it happens is unknown. Research results of partner abuse statistics are controversial. Accusations of misrepresentation and suppression abound. (If you are interested in learning more about research results, take a look at the articles and books listed in Chapter 30, *Resources*.)

Cultural silence about the abuse of men by women, and male training that teaches men that they should be in control, fix problems, and not talk about personal matters, skew research results by undermining men's willingness to report or admit that they are being abused by their female partners.

What I know for sure: abuse of men by women is happening. It's happening a lot, and it has devastating effects—on the men who are the targets of abuse, their children, their friends, co-workers and family, and the women who are abusing.

> "Recognition doesn't hurt anything."

The focus, for the last fifty years, on women's rights and abuse of women by men has made abuse by women a very unpopular topic. Some people actively quash discussion of the topic, as if recognition of abuse *by women* undermines recognition of abuse *of women*. In reality, both are happening, both need attention, and acknowledging one in no way undercuts the other.

As one frustrated abused man put it: "Recognition doesn't hurt anything."

I was at a housewarming party and struck up a conversation with a middle-aged woman who was a friend of my friend. In response to her asking what I do, I mentioned that one of my specialties is the abuse of men by women. She said, "Oh, yeah. I was really abused by my ex-husband." She backed her statement up by describing some major manipulative moves her husband used against her.

After hearing her out, I said, "Actually, my specialty is abuse *of* men *by* women." Her shocked response: "Does that happen?"

Our conversation continued with me explaining some of the ways women abuse men. When I mentioned that one of the ways is purposefully trapping a man with an "unplanned" pregnancy, she said, "That happened to my son!"

She explained, "My son was planning to break up with his girlfriend but came to me crying, saying that she had just told him that she was pregnant. He said he had to do the honorable thing and marry her."

Luckily for this woman's son, his mom was savvy enough to ask if he was sure she was pregnant, and had he gone to any of her doctor's appointments. Her questions instigated her son to question his girlfriend and press that he be allowed to attend her prenatal appointments.

Eventually, the girlfriend revealed that she wasn't really pregnant at all.

This woman had labeled her ex-husband's manipulations as abusive, but had not been able to see the malicious manipulations of her son's girlfriend as abuse until our conversation.

The pendulum doesn't have to swing freely

The women's movement has done a good job of exposing the destruction caused by men abusing women. It has taken the abuse of women by their male partners from being culturally sanctioned and ignored to being widely abhorred. That is as it should be.

But the same has not been done for the abuse of men. In fact, some women treat it as payback.

> A healthy society doesn't condone the abuse of anyone: man, woman, or child.

When I talk to women about the abuse of men by women, sometimes they are surprised, sometimes excited that someone is addressing the issue, and sometimes they are angered that the topic is being given attention.

Sometimes the reaction of women is: "The pendulum just has to swing against men because men have abused women!" The fact that more than once I have heard this comment when talking to other counselors is an unfortunate testament to how widespread and entrenched this attitude is.

Just because some women have been, and are, treated badly by male partners does not mean that it should be open season on men.

The pendulum does *not* have to swing freely until it happens to settle into a balanced position. We are human beings with brains and free will. We can create balance if we choose to.

Anti-male, pro-female climate

We are living in a cultural phase that in many ways is anti-male and pro-female. These stereotyping beliefs and prejudices get in the way of recognizing that women can be abusive towards men, and that those men suffer as a result. They get in the way of people even caring if men get hurt (physically, emotionally, financially…) by women.

A recent American study exposes gender prejudices through a surprising source: the naming of hurricanes.

"Feminine-named hurricanes (vs. masculine-named hurricanes) cause significantly more deaths, apparently because they lead to lower perceived risk and consequently less preparedness. . . . This practice [naming hurricanes with male and female names] also taps into well-developed and widely held gender stereotypes, with potentially deadly consequences."[1]

There is a tendency for men to be thought of as more dangerous than women, for men to be seen as doers of wrong and for women to be seen as innocent.

We tend to blame men for their bad acts. Conversely, we tend to excuse women's bad acts. We assume men do "bad" things because they are "bad." We assume a woman must have had a good reason for doing a "bad" thing. If there is a man even remotely involved, the woman's good reason often loops back to something he did "wrong."

> The guy is responsible for his actions, *and* the guy is responsible for her actions.

It's a double bind for men: the guy is responsible for his actions, *and* the guy is responsible for her actions. If a woman does something wrong, it must be a guy's fault.

In his article "The Gender Paradigm and the Architecture of Antiscience," Dr. Donald Dutton recounts that:

"In March of 2008, ABC News ran a staged sequence in which a man harangued a woman on a public park bench (screamed at her and slapped her). People intervened immediately. When the genders were reversed, no one intervened, and one woman cheered on the female perpetrator because she 'knew he must have done something—cheated or something.'

The Zeitgeist of intimate abuse is thus complete—the abuse is attributed to 'something a man must have done.'"[2]

> *Zeitgeist*:
> "The defining spirit or mood of a particular period of history as shown by the ideas and beliefs of the time"
> —Google definition

It may be that this phenomenon of excusing women's behaviors while holding men responsible is created in part by a desire to get as far away from pre-feminist inequalities as possible. It may be the pendulum swinging freely to the polar opposite.

It may be that excusing women's behavior is left over from long-standing female stereotypes that peg women as so incapable—incapable of being rational, of strength, of fortitude—that we just can't hold them responsible.

We have to get beyond the confines of unfettered cultural backlash and stereotypes so we can see people as they really are and assess behaviors and situations without the blinders of prejudice.

Art imitates life

Patterns in media representations of male-female relationships reflect what's happening culturally. Art imitates life.

> "Have you heard about the woman who stabbed her husband thirty-seven times? I admire her restraint."
> —Roseanne Barr

The abuse of men by women is being presented in movies and television as not only acceptable but amusing and even hysterically funny.

In the trailer for the romantic comedy *Fool's Gold*, Kate Hudson's character hauls off and whacks her ex-husband, played by Matthew McConaughey, in the head with a golf club. This highly abusive act that could easily kill someone is seen as funny. It stimulates laughter. I can't imagine it currently being considered an appropriate story line for a romantic comedy if the genders were reversed.

Men are often portrayed in the media as bumbling idiots that wouldn't know how to tie their shoes if it weren't for a woman standing over them giving them instruction. And it's perfectly acceptable that the instruction be given in a condescending way.

In a Super Bowl 2011 commercial for a low-calorie soda, a woman who appears to be the wife of a man admiring a pie comes up behind the man and abruptly pushes his head into the pie.

In the next scene, she pulls back the shower curtain to expose him hiding, attempting to eat a burger. She grabs the burger out of his mouth and pushes in a bar of soap.

The scene cuts to her sitting down beside him on a park bench. He's drinking the low-calorie soda being promoted in the commercial. She looks at him approvingly, as she is drinking the same beverage herself.

A pretty woman sits down on the next bench. When the man looks at the woman with appreciation, his wife hurls her soda can at him. He ducks and the can hits the pretty woman instead of him. It hits her in the head hard enough to knock her over.

> Women abusing men has become a common story line for selling products.

The wife looks shocked and worried, portraying that she realizes that she could get in trouble for hitting the other woman. The husband and wife run away from the park together.

The wife is worried about getting into trouble for hitting the other woman, but it doesn't seem like she was worried about negative repercussions if she hit her husband with the soda.

This woman is controlling, demanding, humiliating, overly jealous, and physically abusive to her husband, yet the beverage company obviously thought it would attract people to buy their product.

Would a company even contemplate this commercial script if the genders were reversed?

What does it say about our culture that this female-male relationship is seen as something that could leave a good taste in anyone's mouth?

Chapter 2

About partner abuse

Definitions of *abuse*:

"improper or excessive use or treatment: misuse"
—Merriam-Webster.com

"to hurt or injure by maltreatment; ill-use"
—TheFreeDictionary.com

"use or treat in such a way as to cause damage or harm"
—OxfordDictionaries.com

What is partner abuse?

Partner abuse is a pattern of controlling, demeaning, and/or punishing behaviors and attitudes with a dating, cohabiting, or marriage partner, during or after the relationship. At its core, partner abuse is driven by self-centered motivations.

> Partner abuse is a pattern of controlling, demeaning, and/or punishing behaviors and attitudes with self-centered motivations.

It can happen in any configuration of romantic couple, straight or gay. Sometimes a man in a couple abuses his partner, sometimes a woman is abusive, sometimes there is mutual abuse—each partner abusing the other.

We most often think about physically violent acts when we think about partner abuse, but there are many methods of choice for controlling, demeaning, and punishing partners.

Partner abuse takes on many forms. It may be:

- verbal,
- sexual,
- financial,
- physical,
- spiritual,
- legal, or
- emotional/psychological.

Abuse can range from mild to severe. Some behaviors are severely abusive even if they occur only once; others may be considered very abusive because of the number of times they occur. A variety of abusive behaviors may combine to increase the degree of abuse.

Abuse cycle

One of the confusing aspects of partner abuse is that it is often not constant. There can be phases that are more intense and others that are less intense, possibly involving a period of regret, apology, and promises of change.

Sometimes, though not always,* abuse occurs in cycles: increasing tension leading to abuse incident(s), which are followed by a relief of tension, but then tension increases again.

The time period for each part of the cycle is not necessarily the same or consistent. Cycles might occur over months or minutes.

During the *increasing tension* phase, the target of the abuse can be on edge wondering what will set the abusive partner off and when the other shoe will drop.

The *relief of tension* phase may or may not include apologies,** demonstrations of regret, and/or promises of change. Lulls in the abuse may ignite hope that the relationship will improve. This phase may seem absolutely wonderful—the partner may be fun, exciting to be with, and caring—but then there is a return to controlling, demeaning, or punishing behavior.

*In some relationships, tension remains relentlessly high; in others, violent outbursts seem to come out of nowhere.
**An abusive partner may never apologize. When there are apologies, they may be *apologies that aren't apologies*: versions of "I'm sorry I did it, but I wouldn't have done it if you hadn't done _____."

Abusive behavior continuums

Another confusing aspect of partner abuse is deciphering when behavior is "abusive" and when it is "normal." The difference between abusive and healthy behaviors is often found in motivation.

Each potentially abusive behavior can be placed on a continuum which spans from *non-abusive* (totally healthy) to *very abusive*. This spread is one of the things that makes it difficult to determine whether specific behavior is abusive in a specific situation.

non-abusive	very abusive

Everyone gets irritable occasionally. Being abrupt and raising your voice once in a while doesn't meet the criteria for being called abusive. That behavior lands toward the *non-abusive* end of the continuum.

Getting pregnant on purpose without your partner's agreement to become a parent so that you can trap him into marriage is abusive, but not all unplanned pregnancies are on purpose. A truly accidental pregnancy that resulted because reasonable efforts to prevent pregnancy failed would not be considered abusive.

Monitoring a partner's phone and email is abusive if it is obsessive and without rational reason for suspicion, but it may be sensible if trust has been broken and both parties are working together to reestablish the trust. In the second case, the monitoring may be seen as non-abusive.

Examples of behavior continuums:

non-abusive	**YELLING**	very abusive

Non-abusive:
loudly warning someone of immediate danger

Somewhat abusive:
speaking loudly and aggressively about a subject

More abusive:
loud name-calling

Very abusive:
loud, aggressive threats of harm

non-abusive	**PHYSICAL ATTACK**	very abusive

Non-abusive:
attacks made in self-defense

Somewhat abusive:
initiating physical aggression that doesn't result in physical harm or fear of harm

More abusive:
initiating an attack that creates harm or reasonable fear of harm

Very abusive:
murder

Gender bias in determining abuse

If there is a cultural tendency to assign women's actions as most often good and/or men's actions as most often bad, then abuse by a woman against a man may be inappropriately placed on the non-abusive end of the abuse continuum and wrongfully discounted.

For example, in such circumstances, physical attacks by a woman on a man may be seen as being in self-defense even when they are not. Similarly, it may be difficult for a man to recognize that he is being abused because the woman's behaviors are mistakenly excused as warranted by circumstances.

> Where a woman's potentially abusive behavior is placed on the abuse continuum may be distorted by cultural beliefs that:
>
> woman = good
> man = bad
> woman = truth teller
> man = liar

There does appear to be such a cultural bias in North America, and it combines with another set of gender expectations to obscure the abuse of men even further: we tend to believe women and disbelieve men. We expect women to tell the truth and we expect men to distort the truth. This can give unfair weight to women's accusations against men and discount men's accusations against women.

Peter Anderson and Cindy Struckman-Johnson, editors of the book *Sexually Aggressive Women: Current Perspectives and Controversies*, declare that one of the factors getting in the way of research in their topic area is "acceptance of the myth that women can do no harm."[1]

Degrees of abuse

When assessing and understanding abuse in relationships, it's important to take into account both quality and quantity. What a partner does is not the only factor that determines how abusive she is. How often she does it is also a factor.

Frequency of potentially abusive behaviors and attitudes contributes to the impact and degree of abuse. Frequency may be about reoccurrences of the same behavior. It may also be a combination of behaviors. Different mechanisms to control, demean, or punish a partner used in combination can add up to being very abusive.

> Quality and quantity work together to determine the degree of abuse.

A person's collection of behaviors and attitudes in a relationship can be put on an abuse continuum that takes into account the accumulative effect of ways she treats her partner. There are collective degrees or levels of abuse from *non-abusive* to *very abusive*.

| non-abusive | COLLECTIVE | very abusive |

A person can move further towards the *very abusive* end of the collective continuum:

- with a single very abusive act,
- by repeating an abusive act or attitude over and over, or
- by using a number of abusive behaviors and/or attitudes in combination.

For example:

One-time bad act

Non-self-defense stabbing of a partner or ex-partner puts a person on the *very abusive* end of the continuum even if she only does it once.

Repeat offender

Incessantly finding fault every day wears down a partner and can put the fault-finder on the *very abusive* end of the continuum.

The combo

Refusing to contribute to the household financially, withholding sex, name-calling, and insisting that her partner cut ties with his family can all work together to create a very abusive impact.

The collective effect of abusive behaviors is very important to understanding the impact of abuse.

A person on the receiving end of abuse can find it very difficult to explain to other people, and even to himself, why he feels so worn down by the relationship. If he thinks about, or recounts, isolated incidents, things may not seem that bad. The individual incidents might occur in normal healthy relationships. It's the accumulative effect that creates the problem.

One jab might not be much to deal with, but thousands of them doled out daily or intermittently? That's painful and draining. That's abusive.

Book overview

Part One: gave background on abuse of men by women and a rundown of partner abuse in general.

The rest of this book provides details of the who, what, when, where, why, and how of the topic.

Part Two: describes how women abuse their male partners and gives insight into how abuse of men by women is the same as and different from abuse of women by men.

Part Three: presents reasons why abusive women do what they do.

Part Four: explains how men end up in abusive relationships, why they stay, and how the abuse impacts them.

Part Five: helps men who are abused examine their options, whether the relationship continues or ends.

Part Six: delivers a call to action—what everyone (women who are abusing their partners, families of abused men, helping professionals, all men and women) can do about abuse of men by women.

This book is a comprehensive explanation of the topic; you may want to skip around to sections of particular interest to you. Many men who are recovering from being abused by a woman have found that this book helped them digest what had happened to them and helped them move on. They also found that they needed to pace themselves when reading the book so they could process their recognitions and realizations. You may find it helpful to read some sections more than once, possibly with a break in-between readings.

Part Two

Ways women abuse men

How they do it

Sticks and stones may break your bones,
but words may break your psyche,
and overspending may break your finances,
and manipulation may break your spirit,
and . . .

Individuals have methods of choice for demeaning, exerting control over, or punishing the targets of their abuse. The objective is to manipulate situations, the target of the abuse, and even other people relevant to the partner.

Some ways women abuse men are the same as those used in other partner abuse situations, such as isolating the target of abuse from friends and family.

Some ways are similar to those used by men against women but with a twist: women who are physically violent with their male partners are likely to prefer methods that overcome their size and strength disadvantages.

Some abusive behaviors of women are available to them for use on men specifically because of their genders. For example, an abusive woman can capture a man by getting pregnant with his child in a deceitful way.

> Abusive behaviors may cross over different abuse types: seducing a man for malicious purposes using words and body language is verbally, sexually, and psychologically abusive.

Female abuse of male partners includes all the abuse categories:

- verbal
- sexual
- financial
- physical
- spiritual
- legal
- emotional/psychological

Verbal abuse

"What she did was
take all the pain she's ever felt in her whole life
and aim it at me."

Overview

Verbal abuse ranges from rageful to passive aggressive to silent. It can be in-your-face bullying or performed in a more backdoor subversive way. Verbal abuse can achieve its goal to demean, control, or punish loudly or quietly.

Verbal abuse might more properly be called *communication abuse*.

It isn't just words that are the mechanism for abuse. Tone and body language can also be abusive tools.

> Verbal abuse can achieve its goal to demean, control, or punish loudly or quietly.

Verbal abuse instruments cover a broad range:

- threatening
- controlling
- demanding
- histrionics
- fault-finding
- berating
- humiliating
- mocking
- biting sarcasm
- name-calling
- pushing her agenda until he gives in
- circular arguing
- the silent treatment

"Just as assuredly as physical violence assaults the body, verbal abuse assaults the mind and spirit, causing wounds that are extremely difficult to heal." —Beverly Engel, *The Emotionally Abusive Relationship*[1]

Abusive tone and body language

Verbal communication includes tone and body language.

Abusive tone and body language can range from coy to aggressive. A particular woman may use many different forms of tone and body language to demean, control, or punish, or she may have methods of choice that she has honed the art of performing.

Not all incidents of use of the following forms of tone and body language are necessarily "abusive." Motivation is a key to where something gets placed on the continuum measuring the behavior's abusiveness. A woman may cry, pout, or turn away simply because she is sad. She may also cry to control, pout to manipulate, or turn away to punish.

Abusive body language has a variety of forms:

- pouting
- seducing (more on this in Chapter 5, *Sexual Abuse*)
- looking or turning away
- walking away
- aggressively moving towards
- finger-pointing
- withdrawing
- showing a fist
- smirking
- temper tantrums
- crying
- glaring
- menacing
- towering or physically looming over
- eye-rolling
- a demeaning, controlling, or punishing glance

An abusive glance can send a message that the target of the glance has been trained to understand through previous experience. The message may be "You're stupid" or "You better not do that" or "I'm mad at you."

Abusive tone may be any of the following:

- seductive
- fragile
- helpless
- intimidating
- condescending
- loud
- aggressive
- threatening
- silent
- whiny
- coy
- teasing
- charming
- cajoling ("to elicit or obtain by flattery, gentle pleading, or insincere language" OnlineDictionary.com)

A man described the discomfort of attending parties at the home of his kind, well-respected friend: "Stepping in our friend's house was like stepping directly into hell. The air seemed filled with dynamite dust waiting for the right spark to set off an explosion. If someone accidently complimented the host on something, his wife would smirk, roll her eyes, or jump in that person's face until she got a compliment for herself. If someone politely praised one of the dishes prepared by him, "the look" suddenly appeared. Sadly enough, the dinner usually finished in a one-way shouting scene. Guests sat there silently hoping to make themselves invisible. Depending on the situation, crying or temper tantrums became part of the show."

> "If I cannot inspire love,
> I will cause fear."
> —*Frankenstein,*
> Mary Shelley

Threatening

"If you don't do x, you'll be sorry." This type of threat often strikes enough fear to make a partner do whatever "x" is.

Women can use threats to control and punish. Threats may be used to extract compliance to whatever a woman wants to have happen or not happen. They can also be used to burden the target of the threats with fear.

An abusive woman may threaten to:

- be mad or depressed,
- deny access to the children,
- undermine her partner or ex-partner's job,
- expose his secrets,
- cut off sex,
- hurt her partner, herself, the children, or pets,
- end the relationship,
- file false charges,
- fall apart,
- not love him anymore, or
- do anything else she thinks might achieve her goals.

Note that it is *not* abusive for a woman to have reasonable expectations of her partner, to express those expectations tactfully, and to define natural consequences if certain expectations aren't met.

For example, it is *not* abusive for a woman to say to her husband who gets drunk and belligerent every night: "If you don't stop drinking, I'm going to leave you and I will work to not have you be with the children when you have been drinking." This woman has understandable discomfort and concern about her husband's drinking. She has set a reasonable boundary and is taking responsibility for the welfare of herself and her children. While it could be said that this is a threat of consequences if he doesn't meet her demand, it would fall on the *non-abusive* end of the continuum.

On the other hand, unreasonable expectations and demands tied to random threats so she can get her selfish motivations met are abusive. For example, it is abusive for a woman to say to her husband: "If you don't forget about the affair I had, I'll divorce you and good luck seeing the kids," or "You and I both know that you haven't had a drink in two years, but you got that DUI, and if we get divorced I'll have an easy time convincing the court you can't be trusted with the kids!"

Martyrdom is a different twist on threatening. It's a threat made by proxy. The threat is: "I'm carrying such a heavy burden; if you express a problem with me, I'll fall apart." The martyr appears to be so worn out from self-criticism that her partner is deprived of the right to point out problems or concerns he might have with her.

> Martyrdom is threatening's twisted sister.

A man discovered that his wife was having an affair. She claimed she was remorseful and wanted to continue the marriage. She appeared to beat up on herself so much that her husband felt he couldn't express his disappointment or his worry about whether the affair was really over because she was too fragile to witness his pain or address his concerns.

> "Martyrdom covers a multitude of sins."
> —Mark Twain

Controlling

A main objective of abuse is to control. Abusive women can use their words, tone, and/or body language to manipulate and exert control over their partners. Many of the other types of abuse found throughout this section and book describe methods used to exert the control.

A person can control someone in an instant, or over time by wearing them down or conditioning.

Some methods of control are direct and obvious; others may be harder to spot:

- Demands and threats exert control directly.
- Avoidance through withdrawing, redirecting, or outright silence controls by removing the possibility the partner will be able to have his needs met.
- Being seductive, coy, or cajoling through words, tone, and body language are forms of verbal abuse that control in a less obvious way.

Aspects of a man's life an abusive woman may try to control include:

- time,
- space,
- activity,
- contact with other people,
- access to resources,
- appearance, and even
- opinion and thought.

Demanding

With demanding, there is a "do it or else" attitude. There is a rigidity. It's "my way or the highway."

A demanding woman has unreasonable expectations of her partner and her requests for compliance are followed up with extracting a price if he doesn't live up to those expectations. The price paid may be having to deal with her anger, silence, or pouting.

The nagging wife or girlfriend is the classic picture of a demanding woman. Unfortunately, the classic picture includes women who have reasonable expectations and frustrations.

It is *not* demanding for a woman to tactfully express reasonable expectations or frustration that her reasonable expectations aren't being met, and to initiate conversations about her and her partner's thoughts and attitudes about the situation.

It is demanding for her to set unreasonable standards and rules on her own, impose them on her partner, and punish him for not living up to her standards and rules.

demanding	not demanding
he needs to fill the dishwasher at a certain time in a certain way or there is hell to pay	she tells him it isn't OK that filling the dishwasher keeps becoming her responsibility even though he keeps saying he'll take care of it
he needs to come home straight after work, no exceptions, or she gives him the silent treatment	she tells him that it isn't OK with her that he goes out with the guys many nights after work while she's taking care of the kids

Histrionics

Histrionics are behaviors that are overly emotional and melodramatic. Women who are histrionic keep their partners busy trying to put out fires or preempt them in order to avoid the overreactions.

Life with a histrionic woman is chaotic and drama-drenched; minor problems are blown up into major catastrophes:

- Being frustrated with her wardrobe stimulates an episode of yelling, throwing clothes from her closet onto the floor, and refusal to attend a party.
- Having a meal not turn out as planned precipitates a theatrical show of the dinner being thrown into the trash and stomping off to bed, leaving the family to fend for themselves.

> *Super-crying*
> is
> over-the-top crying
> that a woman uses
> to get what she wants.

Super-crying is an example of histrionics. It's over-the-top crying that serves to get a woman what she wants. It's often used to end a conversation about a subject she wants to avoid or to divert attention. It can be used to punish her partner for having even tried to have a conversation about something important to him.

Several men have recounted stories of being met with super-crying when they tried to talk to their wives about finances. In each case, the women controlled the money, and in each case it was eventually exposed that bills weren't paid or money was missing. The crying achieved the goal of shutting down the husband's ability to discover the financial manipulations.

Fault-finding

People get to point out problems they have with their partner. The delivery, frequency, and legitimacy of criticism are factors that determine where pointing out problems falls on the abusiveness continuum.

With fault-finding, people are actively seeking something to accuse their target of. There is a desire to show the target to be bad, sick, stupid, or crazy.

Abusive people often minimize their own mistakes while maximizing any made by the target of their abuse. They can get satisfaction out of zinging their partner with criticism, accusations, negative judgments, or blaming.

Fault-finding has many forms:

- criticism
- accusations
- negative judgments
- blaming
- exaggerating his mistakes and shortcomings
- fabrication (making things up in order to have something to criticize)
- capitalizing on his vulnerabilities using any of the methods listed above
- minimizing her faults
- abdicating responsibility (making everything his fault)
- apologies for her "bad" behavior that turn into blaming him for her actions
- making him responsible for decisions then criticizing the outcome
- projecting her own "bad" behaviors onto him

The fault-finding doesn't necessarily have to be based in reality; sometimes abusive people exaggerate their partners' mistakes or shortcomings, or they just make stuff up.

> A *fault-reversal apology* starts with "I'm sorry," then moves on to the "but you made me do it" part.

If a man has an abusive female partner, he may find that even when something is her fault, she manages to blame him: "Look what you made me do!" or "I wouldn't have done it if you hadn't _____."

An abusive partner may abdicate responsibility for decision-making and then turn on you when the decision produces something she can find fault with. It puts you in a "damned if you do, damned if you don't" position.

Sometimes fault-finding is *projection*. Like a movie projector projecting pictures onto a screen, people can project their own negative behaviors onto someone else. They accuse the other person of having the undesirable qualities they themselves have, or doing the "bad" behaviors they themselves do.

Examples of projection:

- A woman falsely accused her husband of being unfaithful when she was the one having an affair.
- A woman whose husband tactfully and gently asked her to engage in a conversation about the finances stood up and yelled at him, "I'm not going to stick around and be yelled at by you!"
- A woman berated her husband for being uncaring, while he went out of his way to take care of her and the family and she selfishly put herself first.

Berating

Berating is an intense, angry put-down. Other words and terms used to describe berating include:

- harshly criticize,
- rebuke,
- tear into,
- blast,
- condemn vehemently,
- scold at length, and
- eviscerate.

When I think of berating, I think of demeaning criticism that cuts you down and is particularly difficult to endure. You desperately want it to stop. It is extremely condescending and has an intensely shaming aspect to it.

> "She is so busy jumping to conclusions that it's how she gets her exercise."

The criticisms may stem from:

- actual occurrences,
- minor infractions or mistakes that are blown out of proportion,
- assumptions on her part,
- things she imagines, or
- stuff she makes up.

One man's description of his wife's berating activity: "She is so busy jumping to conclusions that it's how she gets her exercise."

Humiliating

When someone sets out to humiliate another person, she works to shame, degrade, and embarrass him. Humiliation is a particularly brutal type of abuse as the feeling of being betrayed heaps more wounding on top of the shame, embarrassment, and fear.

Romantic relationships create unique vulnerabilities to humiliation because:

- there is a natural longing to be respected by your partner;
- your partner has access to friends, family, co-workers, and other people you want to think well of you;
- your partner is often privy to your secrets; and
- it is difficult to defend yourself against false accusations about things that occur in private.

A woman may humiliate her partner in private through demeaning and belittling comments, accusing him of having traits that she knows go against his values, or by attacking him about something from his past that he already has shame about.

> As one man put it: "The person who would know your wounds and use them as stabbing points is not your *partner.*"

Public humiliation can be used by an abusive woman to demean a current partner or punish an ex after the relationship ends. The stories she uses to humiliate may or may not be true.

A man described his abusive wife's propensity to publicly humiliate him: "No event seemed safe when attending as a couple. With time, I despised showing up at social functions, parties, and family gatherings. Being a very bright lady, the Ex would artfully manage to introduce her distorted stories about me into conversations with friends, acquaintances, or even complete strangers.

If a woman was caught bragging about her husband's good deeds, often with misty eyes and deep sighs, the Ex would complement the spouse and then tell her how lucky a woman she was in comparison to her. In front of friends and relatives, I was a constant target and openly accused of never doing or saying anything right. If cold looks and mistrust could kill, I would have died a long time ago."

Social media extends the reach of an abusive woman intent on humiliating her target. She might post pictures without consent, spread lies or rumors, pretend she is her partner or ex-partner online, or send disparaging texts or emails.

The National Crime Prevention Council says cyberbullying happens "when the Internet, cell phones, or other devices are used to send or post text or images intended to hurt or embarrass another person."[2]

An abusive woman may expand her circle of humiliation to include people that her partner or ex-partner cares about or is associated with.

A woman got a call late at night from a friend. The friend had just received an email accusing the woman of having had sex with the friend's husband several years prior. The email was sent by the woman's boyfriend's ex-girlfriend. (It's challenging to follow this cavalcade of characters.)

The ex-girlfriend sent the email to the adult children of both her ex-boyfriend and his new girlfriend, as well as other family members and friends. The story wasn't true or believed, but the couple felt terrorized by the ex's efforts.

Mocking

There is a taunting quality to mocking. It involves making fun of someone. It shows a lack of respect for the targeted person. When the mocking is witnessed by the target's children, friends, co-workers, or family, it is particularly stinging and embarrassing.

Teasing can run off course and be unintentionally hurtful, but mocking is intentionally (subconsciously or consciously) demeaning. It can result in the mocked person feeling incompetent, inadequate, and inherently flawed.

Mocking men has become an American pastime. It's a sport. It is entertainment. Commercials, movies, and TV sitcoms depict men as stupid, inept, and unable to take care of themselves without the help of a woman.

A woman who mocks her partner or ex-partner may be doing it for the sport of it, or she may be trying to provoke him in order to entrap him so she can call him abusive or get a restraining order.

One man's wife had a repertoire of imaginary inadequacies she repeatedly mocked her husband about. She was particularly fond of mocking him about what she saw as his lack of ability to do manly things. In front of friends and family she would make comments like, "He's useless in practical things" and "You know how useless he is."

This man worked very hard. He had a successful career and did most of the household work as well. He had done plenty of manly things, like building a porch on his house. Despite all the evidence that he wasn't "useless," his wife made her negative comments so often that he began to believe them.

Biting sarcasm

Humor is a wonderful thing. It can increase the joy in life and make difficult circumstances easier to deal with. Sarcasm is an art form that can be fun and witty.

Biting sarcasm, while it may be witty, is not fun for the target. Biting sarcasm is a backdoor way of getting in a dig.

The *sarcaser* (person who expressed the biting sarcasm) acts like they are getting away with the dig against the *sarcasee* (subject of the biting sarcasm) because it is couched in humor.

The sarcasee generally feels hurt and confused, with little ability to address the impact of the sarcasm because, after all, "It was just a joke."

A person that uses sarcasm in a healthy way looks for cues indicating how the subject of the sarcasm reacted. If there are markers that feelings were hurt, then they've gone too far and need to back off. Apologies may be appropriate.

Anyone who uses sarcasm and responds with "You're too sensitive" when the targets of the sarcasm complain that their feelings were hurt is not able to use sarcasm in a healthy way.

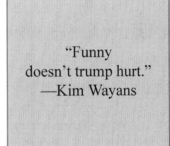

"Funny doesn't trump hurt."
—Kim Wayans

In healthy sarcasm, the desire to be funny isn't more important than the target person's feelings.

Name-calling

In healthy relationships, when you have disagreements you have the goal of getting an understanding of each other's point of view and working together to a resolution. Name-calling is the antithesis of that.

> "If you can't answer a man's arguments, all is not lost; you can still call him vile names."
> —Elbert Hubbard

Name-calling can pack an intense verbal punch. It is particularly demeaning when it misrepresents the target of the attack. Name-calling often lumps the targets of the abuse in with types of people they don't want to be. Men can find it particularly painful to be called names that attack their manhood or names that categorize them with the type of man they have worked hard to not be.

A man scurried to gather some of his belongings before moving out of his marital home the day after his wife physically attacked him. As he walked out the front door, his wife yelled at him loud enough so that the neighbors could hear: "Get out of here, you cheater!"

He hadn't cheated on her. He'd never cheated on her. It went against his values and his actions. The verbal slap was meant to demean and humiliate him, and discredit him in the eyes of the neighbors.

A different incident of name-calling could be placed toward the other end, the *non-abusive* end, of the abuse continuum. A woman called her husband "a jerk" once, following her discovery that he had done quite a jerky thing. She apologized to him shortly after saying it and worked at talking to him about her concerns in a healthier way.

Pushing and Circling

One way to "win" a fight is to never stop fighting until your opponent capitulates. You just wear him down. He may not be genuinely convinced that you have the better idea, but he stops resisting.

Pushing her agenda until he gives in can happen in a belligerent, aggressive way or in a more persistent, slow, and quiet way.

Women who use this tactic may mistakenly think that they have won their partner over to see things the same as they do. Meanwhile, the partner adds it to the list of times he doesn't feel heard or taken into consideration.

Circular arguing is illogical arguing that goes around and around and makes the listener's head spin trying to track what the person is saying. It is difficult to follow the trail of the argument because it isn't rational and loops back on itself.

When a woman uses circular arguing with her partner, she takes control of the communication. The partner goes into a deer-in-the-headlights trance, not knowing how to respond. There isn't anywhere to take the conversation. It's just over.

Circular arguing can look like: "You wanted me to do that thing today. The sky is blue today. I can't do that thing when the sky is blue." The listener knows that the "thing" has nothing to do with weather or sky color, and is left dazed and confused by the unreasonable argument.

Synonyms for
the silent treatment:

give the cold shoulder
ignore
ostracize
shun
make unwelcome
neglect
snub
look through
avoid
spurn

The silent treatment

Abuse isn't always in-your-face loud. It may be the exact opposite. An abusive person may go silent or sulk when she is angry with her partner or she wants attention. Extended silence can be punishing, demeaning, and controlling.

The silent treatment is different from a partner taking a break from a conversation to collect her thoughts or avoid saying something she may regret later.

There is a torturous aspect to the silent treatment. The target often feels rejected and inadequate. It puts him through the torture of guessing what set her off.

The silent treatment can:

- win arguments by shutting out the opposition,
- boost the silent partner's ego because it keeps the shunned partner focused on the silent partner, and
- send the loud and clear message that the targeted partner is so bad, sick, stupid, or crazy that he isn't worthy of his partner's attention.

The target of the silent treatment has a very difficult time getting people to understand how terrible the experience is for him. It is very challenging to prove that you are being treated in this way. He is trying to put his finger on something that is *not* happening. It is difficult to prove a negative.

Chapter 5

Sexual abuse

"Contrary to stereotypes
that women are sexually passive and 'uninterested,'
there are women who demand, pressure, extort, and even
force adult and adolescent men into sexual interactions."

—Peter Anderson and Cindy Struckman-Johnson,
*Sexually Aggressive Women:
Current Perspectives and Controversies*

Overview

In sexual abuse, sex is the mechanism for abuse.

People can be shocked at the idea that women can sexually abuse men, but women can, and do, sexually abuse men. It may look different than the classic sexual abuse of women by men, but it is sexual abuse when a woman uses sex in a controlling, demeaning, or punishing way, and/or uses sex to control, demean, or punish.

> Sexual abuse of men may occur during any phase or type of relationship:
> a one-night-stand,
> dating,
> cohabitating,
> marriage,
> or after a break-up.

The control exerted may be directly regarding the time, place, and methods of sexual activity, or it may be about the results of sexual activity. The control may be regarding non-sexual areas of life, but sex is the tool used for control.

There are many ways a woman might sexually abuse a male partner:

- forcing or pressuring him into sexual activities
- withholding sex
- using sex as a manipulation tool
- using sex to lure and trap
- "accidental" or coerced pregnancy
- flirting or having affairs with other men
- sexual teasing
- seduction
- belittling sexual performance
- false accusations of rape/sexual abuse

Forcing/pressuring him into sexual activities

We have a cultural expectation that men are supposed to want sex whenever they can get it, in whatever form it's offered, as long as it's with a partner of a gender they are attracted to.

But when you really examine that stereotype, it doesn't hold up. While men may be prewired to have a strong sex drive, that doesn't mean that they are without limits on what they want in the way of sexual activity.

The stereotype that says "a man wants sex all the time" sets men up for being made fun of when they don't fit that unrealistic stereotype. A woman can use this or other means to pressure a man to have sex, go further than he wants to, or engage in certain sexual activities he doesn't want to engage in.

Males aren't the only people with sex drive. Females have a drive for sex also. Any particular female's desire for sex may or may not be less than a particular man's. Some women's sex drive isn't as constant as the typical man's but creates strong surges of desire. Those surges of desire might not match with their potentially available partner's interest in sex at that time.

Some men don't want to get involved sexually with women too quickly in a new relationship. They may have been burnt before by the hormonal fog that clouds ability to see people for who they really are once you bring sex into the relationship. They may have other reasons for not wanting to fast-forward sex. These men often find themselves pressured for sex by their dating partners. It may be unwanted touching. Unwanted touching may be just the beginning. It may be more aggressive moves.

In a healthy relationship, there are times when each partner initiates sex, putting some effort into arousing the other partner's interest, while respecting the partner's wishes about time, place, and types of sexual activity. The initiator stops pursuit if they receive signals that there just isn't going to be interest this time. Healthy partners can talk about sex and one person's desires and wishes don't trump the other person's desires and wishes.

When a woman abusively forces or pressures a partner for sex, she may be motivated in part by sexual desire, but she is also driven by desire to demean, control, or punish.

The controlling element may be directly related in that she is demanding sex at a particular time, place, or way without regard for what her partner wants.

The forcing or pressuring may be physical, or it may be psychological or emotional. The forcing or pressuring may be created by there being a cost extracted or threatened if her partner doesn't comply. The cost may be that she:

- shames or humiliates him,
- makes his life miserable, or
- threatens the end of the relationship or that she won't love him anymore.

A woman may set up a compromising situation for her sexual target or take advantage of a man who is in a vulnerable situation or state. His ability to resist may be compromised by him being:

- intoxicated or drugged,
- isolated,
- asleep or exhausted, or
- pinned down.

In their book *Sexually Aggressive Women: Current Perspectives and Controversies*, Peter Anderson and Cindy Struckman-Johnson explain:

> Unwanted sexual touching may stimulate a biological response in a man even when he is not psychologically or emotionally interested in the sexual activity.

"We define female heterosexual aggression as an act in which a woman uses pressure or force to obtain sexual contact with an adolescent or adult man against his will.

Our contributing authors have documented that only small percentages of women use force tactics such as physical restraint, the threat or use of physical harm, or the use of weapons. For the most part, our contributors are writing about women who have used pressure tactics such as verbal demands, emotional manipulation, deception, blackmail, and intoxication to gain sexual access to reluctant men."[1]

A man found that after they were married, his wife only wanted sex in the early morning. He worked long hours. He was tired in the morning. He didn't want to have sex at that time of day. She ignored his objections. She'd just get on top of him and basically force a biological reaction.

She didn't care whether he was asleep or awake. There was no romance. No intimacy. No consideration of his opinion. It was humiliating to him. It was just one of the many ways that his wife was controlling and demanding.

Another man, Alan, is quoted on the Australian website One In Three: "Her sexual violation of my reluctant body had no name. Her demands were not simply an occasional inconsiderate insistence. This was a remorseless and frightening menace."

Withholding sex

It is not unusual for a woman's desire for sex to be stronger sometimes and weaker other times. Normal healthy relationships can have spans of time when there isn't much sex. A woman's libido may be low because of exhaustion, stress, illness, or hormone swings. She may lack interest in sex because of strain in the relationship.

Withholding sex is different than not being in the mood for sex or not feeling close enough to a partner to feel interested in sex. Abusive withholding of sex is driven by self-centeredness, lack of caring about her partner, or a desire to punish.

Typical rules of engagement in committed relationships include monogamy. That means that if there isn't sex inside the relationship, there isn't sex at all. That can be a painful position for a man to be in.

Besides being sexually frustrated, a man who is in a sexless marriage or relationship may feel:

- rejected,
- unattractive,
- not good enough,
- inadequate,
- undesirable, and/or
- shamed for having sexual desires.

A young man felt constantly denied by his demanding wife. They had sex about once every three weeks. He got confusing signals from her—ask, don't ask—either choice was met with criticism. This went on for years. The marriage ended shortly after she poured salt on the wound by having a sexual relationship with a male acquaintance.

Using sex as a manipulation tool

A woman can use sex as a manipulation tool by flipping between withholding sex to coerce or punish and using sex as a reward for desired behavior. The promise of sex can be a powerful enticement for a man.

There is a reason why there is a common North American term (which I prefer not to use here in its usual form) that is the equivalent of "vaginally whipped." The saying describes a man that is compelled to comply with his mate's many and irrational demands in order to maintain sexual access to her.

> The messages to the vaginally whipped are: "If you comply, you'll be rewarded with sex." "If you don't do as I say, you'll be cut off."

I always hated the vulgar version of "vaginally whipped," thinking that it was an undeserved slam on women. Then I met women who used sex to manipulate their partners into giving in to their every whim, using sex as both the carrot and stick, the reward and punishment. Now I understand why the saying exists.

The tantalizing carrot is, "If you comply, you'll be rewarded with sex (or you'll get pleasure in a certain way)." The menacing stick is, "If you don't do as I say, you'll be cut off."

One man explained how this played out in his marriage:

> "I was sexually inexperienced when we met. She came on strong, sexually teasing me. She used sex to trap me. After we were married, sex was less and less. If I was 'a good boy,' she'd give sex. If I was 'a bad boy,' she'd withhold it. I eventually stopped initiating it. I was relieved when I went on antidepressants and they made my libido go down."

Using sex to lure and trap

Merriam-Webster.com defines *lure* as:

1. an object usually of leather or feathers attached to a long cord and used by a falconer to recall or exercise a hawk
2. a: an inducement to pleasure or gain, enticement
   b: appeal, attraction
3. a decoy for attracting animals to capture, as
   a: artificial bait used for catching fish
   b: an often luminous structure on the head of pediculate fish that is used to attract prey

While the second definition is a direct fit for defining a woman luring a man with sex, the first and third definitions are interesting for drawing parallels between what happens to humans and how lures are used with animals. Terms like "a decoy for attracting animals to capture" and "used to attract prey" and the description of a lure made of "leather or feathers" all strongly parallel the human experience of being lured by sex.

The availability for sex may be alluring in and of itself, or a woman may set a particularly enticing trap by being very sexual or acting out a man's sexual fantasies. This is most often deployed during dating or whenever the relationship is at risk of ending.

Sometimes, after a woman traps a man with sex she then denies him sexual activity—the lure and trap turns into a bait and switch.

A man had known a woman for a very short time when they began having wild, passionate sex. She instigated these encounters frequently and was eager to fulfill his sexual fantasies. He was thrilled to find such a partner. She had other attributes and personality traits that he admired and he was excited to marry her.

After they were married and had a child, things were different. Lack of sex became a permanent condition of the marriage. She was very demeaning about his desire for more physical intimacy. She was also bullying and controlling in other ways—attributes he hadn't noticed until after they were married.

Another man was drawn into a relationship with a woman who said she wanted the same sexual activities he longed for. His sexual fantasies weren't dangerous or violent, just not what every partner would necessarily want. He was thrilled to find a partner with the same sexual interests.

She participated in the acting out of his sexual fantasies once, and then she said she would only be comfortable doing that again when they were in a committed relationship. They moved in together and commingled their finances, and he helped her raise her son, but mysteriously (to him anyway), she still never wanted to engage in those sexual activities again.

With the sexual bait and switch a woman's secret intention is: "Once I've got him, it'll be different."

Normal relationships often start off with a heat that is not sustainable. The sexual bait and switch is different from the normal ebbs and flows of sexual interest in a long-term relationship. Sexual bait and switch involves intentional use of sex to trap along with the premeditated thought that "Once I've got him, it'll be different."

"Accidental" or coerced pregnancy

Pregnancy is a very effective way of trapping a man. It can trap him into a relationship, marriage, and/or child support. A self-centered woman may abuse a man's reproductive rights in order to trap him, or for the opposite result—she may use a man to get her pregnant because she wants a child, then push the father out of the child's life.

A woman may:

- manipulate a man into giving in to her desires to have a child even if he doesn't want one,
- get pregnant on purpose and claim it was accidental,
- pretend to be pregnant when she isn't, or
- use a partner as a sperm donor.

A woman who pretends to be pregnant when she isn't may also pretend to have a miscarriage after she has secured the trap with a marriage certificate.

Accidental pregnancies are common. It can be very challenging to figure out whether it was accidentally-on-purpose or whether reasonable precautions against pregnancy were taken and failed.

> A woman may "pull the goalie" by secretly not taking her birth control pills or sabotaging contraceptive attempts.

Men can be at a disadvantage for deciphering whether the story of how a woman became accidentally pregnant is true, because men don't typically know that much about the details of how conception and contraception work. They have the basic concepts, but women can often come up with a cover story that men don't have enough background information to question.

Common excuses for getting pregnant accidentally-on-purpose include "forgetting" to take birth control pills, or having to go off them for some reason, and then for some other reason not using another type of birth control at all or successfully. Then it's, "Oops. *We're* having a baby."

To trick an unwilling man into becoming a dad, some women will put pin holes in condoms, or convince him in the heat of the moment that they don't need to be using safe sex methods even though she knows it is a risky time in her cycle.

In the first chapter, I mentioned a woman whose son had come to her crying, devastated by the news that the girlfriend he had planned to break up with was pregnant. He felt he had to do the honorable thing and marry her. The mom was able to counsel her son to investigate the legitimacy of the girlfriend's pregnancy claim.

Her claim didn't stand up to scrutiny, and her deceitful attempt to trap her boyfriend was exposed. No doubt, she knew he was about to break up with her and decided she needed to close the deal immediately.

Another man was pressured by his wife to have a child together immediately after they married. He wanted to wait a year, but she didn't care. She complained that her IUD was uncomfortable so she had it taken out. She said that condoms got in the way of her sexual enjoyment, so she refused their use. It wasn't long before she got her wish.

A different man's wife didn't even try to create a cover story. Even though he had been clear that he didn't want any more children, she simply announced one day that she had stopped taking birth control without his knowledge and was pregnant with their third child.

Flirting or having affairs with other men

Sometimes people find themselves attracted to a person who isn't their current partner. Sometimes they have affairs outside of their current relationships. These activities enter the realm of abuse when there is a controlling, demeaning, or punishing motivation behind the behavior.

After breaking up with his girlfriend, a man received a text ostensibly sent to him by mistake. It was from his ex-girlfriend, supposedly intended for one of his close male friends. (Let's call the friend Mark.)

The text read as intimate conversation between his ex and friend. It tore the man apart that his friend was getting it on with his ex, especially so soon after their breakup.

The "mistake" text was only the beginning. His ex would call him in the middle of the night to chat and just happen to say things like "I just left Mark's." Each time, it was like a knife stabbing the man's heart. He was in turmoil.

He wondered if he should try to win her back, until he finally got it that her actions were part of a larger pattern of manipulative, demanding, and controlling behaviors on her part and that he was much better off without her.

A different woman recounted that she and her husband would both use flirting to try to hurt each other when they were fighting. If they were in a bar during an argumentative phase, the angry partner would very publicly flirt with random bar patrons, intentionally trying to create pain for the other partner in order to punish him/her.

Seduction and Sexual teasing

Seduction and sexual teasing can be playful activities enjoyed by both parties. On the other hand, a woman's abusive seduction and sexual teasing are games where the objective isn't a shared experience. The objective is to feed her desire to have power and control, especially over a man.

An abusive woman may seduce men to get them to do whatever it is she wants them to do:

- have sex with her
- buy her things
- give in to her wishes
- commit to a relationship
- pursue her

A man's female co-worker seduced him into a sexual relationship, then used the power that gave her to make him support her work aspirations. Whenever she wanted his backing on her ideas, she would threaten to go to the company administration and cause problems for him.

Travis Alexander was tragically murdered by his ex-girlfriend Jodi Arias. Jodi appears to have used seduction to capture Travis, to recapture him whenever he pulled away from the relationship, and to set him up to do him harm the last day they were together.

Abusive sexual teasing revs a guy up with the intention of leaving him hanging. It's different from having second thoughts about getting sexual. It's done for the sheer fun of manipulating a man. A woman who abuses men in this way enjoys seeing them "want" her, and enjoys the pain it inflicts. It feeds her ego.

Belittling sexual performance

In healthy relationships, both partners can talk about their sexual preferences. They can share their fantasies with the expectation that their private conversations about such personal information will be kept private and met with understanding even if the other partner doesn't wish to participate in the enactment of those fantasies.

Healthy partners can tactfully let each other know how the other is doing in stimulating and satisfying their sexual desires: "A little to the left." "A little to the right." "Slower." "Faster." "I'd like some more foreplay." "This is the kind of foreplay I like . . ."

Abusive comments and attitudes about a partner's sexual performance aren't compassionate or understanding. An abusive woman may make demeaning comments to her partner about his:

- body or appearance,
- sexual performance,
- sexual desirability,
- fantasies, or
- lack of desire to participate in sexual activities he finds repulsive or demeaning.

An abusive woman may shame her partner for simply having a normal healthy level of desire for sex. (It's *not* abusive for a woman to draw the line against an excessive amount of sex. I'm not talking about a woman tactfully telling her partner she doesn't want to have sex every day, or at inopportune times; I'm talking about women who demean their partners for having a normal guy level of sexual desire.)

False accusations of rape/sexual abuse

False accusations of rape, sexual assault, or sexual abuse are devastating to innocent men. False accusation of sexual abuse is sexual abuse. A woman who falsely accuses a man of sexually abusing her or their children is sexually abusing that man.

> False accusation of sexual abuse is sexual abuse of the falsely accused.

Not every woman that says she was raped or sexually assaulted was actually raped or sexually assaulted. Not every woman that says her partner sexually abused their child is telling the truth. There are many potential subconscious reasons or conscious motivations why an individual woman might distort or contrive a claim against an individual man.

A man's estranged wife tried to get the upper hand in a custody battle by accusing him of sexual abuse. She first accused him of tickling their daughter until she cried. The inference was that the "tickling" was sexually motivated. Her follow-up accusation was that while they were married he tried talking her into having sex with animals.

The man was blindsided by the accusations: "I know that nothing even remotely close to the tickling accusation ever happened. The animal thing is a complete fabrication. Why say things like that? Why try to destroy me? It's cruel!"

Another man devastated by his wife's false accusation of sexual abuse described his torment: "It's the worst thing anyone could accuse me of, sexual abuse. I find it terrible to be lumped in with those men. I'm repulsed by men who do what she accused me of."

6 Chapter

Financial abuse

"Every night, I'd walk in and be so tired
and she wouldn't say hi.
She'd smile and say, 'Checks, please.'"

Overview

When people focus on financial ways men abuse women, they often talk about men who exert control by limiting their partner's ability to work or access to family money. While those same abuses may occur when the genders are flipped, there also are financial abuses that are available for women to use against men that take advantage of traditional gender roles.

A woman might be in a position to control finances because she has a much larger income than her partner. Another woman may take advantage of a man's role as "provider" by demanding he provide an unreasonable amount or in unreasonable ways. If he doesn't live up to her demands, there is a price to pay. The same woman, or other women, may capitalize on female gender roles to help her avoid financial responsibility.

The female-on-male financial abuse ways and means are diverse:

> "She's madly in love with wallets, not people!"

- getting him to buy her things
- controlling the finances
- restricting access to financial information
- demanding he make more money
- misuse of funds
- stealing from him or the family
- ruining his credit
- keeping the family financially burdened
- refusing to contribute financially to the family
- limiting his ability to work
- destroying his property

Getting him to buy her things

Male gender-role training that says men need to prove they can provide financially for their partner and potential, or actual, family sets men up to be vulnerable to women who wish to take advantage of them financially.

Though women have made great strides in equal rights with men, such as vastly increased occupation choices, many still have hung on, with a death grip, to unequal rights that favor women. Men paying for everything—from dinner, to diamonds, to literally *everything*—is a vestige of the old days that some women love to capitalize on.

Many men are conditioned to not question their role as gift-giver, and can't quite put their finger on what feels so awful if they are taken advantage of in this way. If they do consciously think it's unfair, they may be ashamed to admit it, or find little support for their view.

A man's girlfriend often travelled internationally for her jewelry business. She talked him into giving her money to purchase her engagement ring on one of her trips by convincing him that she could get a great deal through her contacts. She came back from the trip with a diamond ring and all seemed good with the world.

Imagine his shock, then, when her husband showed up at his door one day. This fiancée to him, wife of another man, didn't travel for business. That was her cover story for not being available all the time. How much of his money she pocketed and how much she spent on her "engagement" ring is unknown, but certainly neither was returned to him.

Controlling and Restricting

Some women may control their family's finances because they are the major earners of their family, but even if a woman is not bringing in the bulk of the family income, or any income, she may still control the family purse strings.

A man may be convinced that his partner has more time or ability to manage the budget and then find that he has less and less access to funds or ability to make reasonable purchases, or a woman may take control more directly.

In situations where a couple recognizes that the woman genuinely has a better history with handling money and they have agreed that it is in everyone's financial best interests that he have limited access because he has a spending problem, then her control of the funds may be healthy and warranted.

In abusive situations, a woman may gradually or quickly take control of the finances, limit her partner's input into how money will be spent, and restrict his access to financial information. She may use any combination of coercion, control, manipulation, or humiliation to secure her hold on the money.

> An abusive woman may use any combination of coercion, control, manipulation, or humiliation to secure her hold on the money.

In Chapter 1, *Women abuse men? Does that happen?*, I mentioned a man who only found out after separation that he and his estranged wife had several years of unpaid taxes. He had given her the money to pay the taxes each year. He thought she had paid the taxes each year. But she had not.

He had trusted her to handle the family finances and the bookkeeping for his business. He was run ragged with the physical demands of the business and she appeared to be taking care of the bills. Occasionally, he had attempted to get more information about how things were going financially, but she would either divert his attention or accuse him of creating too much work for her.

His wife spent lavishly on herself while she always talked him out of buying weather-appropriate gear he needed for his work or anything else he wanted. His requests for some of the income from his business were met with an emotionally laden litany of excuses why they couldn't afford the purchase.

She always managed to convince him there wasn't enough money to go around, so he had to sacrifice for the family. He described the feeling he had, after years of the same money-for-her/none-for-him scenarios repeating over and over, as "frugal fatigue."

During his divorce, it took forensic accounting to weed through the tangled mess his wife had made of the business and personal financial records. The digging uncovered that over a year prior to any talk of separation, she had funneled money from his business into an undisclosed account.

To add insult to injury—or more accurately, injury to injury—after the divorce settlement left them each responsible for half of the back taxes, the ex-wife filed for Innocent Spouse with the IRS. Despite the very strong documentation the man submitted to the IRS to refute her claim, the IRS awarded her Innocent Spouse status, making him responsible to pay all the tax debt the couple had incurred while together.

Demanding he make more money

Men typically want to be a good provider for their partner and family. It's part of cultural expectations for a man and a major source of self-esteem.

An abusive woman can take advantage of her partner's desire to be a good provider by making unreasonable demands and coercing compliance through crying, pouting, yelling . . ., or by rewarding her partner with sex.

A man was talked into buying a home that was much larger and more expensive than he thought wise, necessary, or practical. After the purchase, his wife worked less and less at her business. He struggled with the burden of making the mortgage payments on his own.

Time and again, he instigated conversations with his wife about his concerns. Each time, she maneuvered around the subject. His concerns grew bigger and bigger. Finally, he pushed through and insisted they talk about it.

His wife became despondent. She said that she *needed* the stability of the home and couldn't bear to move. The only thing that would console her was his agreement to let go of his idea to sell the house. Feeling sorry for her, he took on more business, upping his hours to ten hours, seven days a week, to try to make ends meet.

Eventually, the housing market took its downturn and opportunity to sell the house evaporated. The wife continued spending money on herself but stopped sending the mortgage payments. She left him for another man right as the house was about to be foreclosed.

Misuse of funds

There are many ways that a woman might misuse joint or her partner's funds and then leave him holding the bag:

- gambling
- shopping addiction
- hiding her spending
- buying things they can't afford
- lying about paying bills
- buying drugs or alcohol
- racking up credit card debt
- rerouting funds into her private account
- thwarting repayment of loans from his family

If his partner has a shopping or gambling addiction, a man may try to reason with her about her spending too much, but she will maneuver around him in order to get her fix. With any form of addiction, an addict will lie and manipulate to get her substance. A woman may use anger or crying to shut her partner down if he tries to reason with her; she may beguile him with how she needs him to provide things for her, or she may simply ignore his pleas.

A professional man with a well-paying position but large debt load that restricted his disposable income had tried many times to talk to his wife about cutting down her spending. Her consistent response was that she would continue to spend whatever she wanted. She threatened that if he didn't stop bothering her about it, she would leave and take the children.

I have heard many stories of men finding out bills they thought were being paid by their wife, who took care of that responsibility for the family, were not actually being paid.

One man found out his child support payments related to children from his previous marriage had not been paid, even though his wife had led him to believe that they were being paid on time.

Another man's new wife convinced him that she should take care of the family finances. She said, "You work hard and make the money. I'm good at accounting. I'll take care of it."

She occasionally showed him some financial records, but only occasionally. They had a huge house that they paid off faster than the mortgage demanded. They had investments that she organized for them.

Actually, he thought the investments were for "them," but they were in her name. Somehow, she managed to get a clause put on the investments that in the case of separation they were all hers. He didn't realize he needed to be protecting himself from his wife. He trusted she was taking care of these things with both their interests in mind.

His wife took advantage of the fact that he was consumed by juggling his career, housework, and the kids. He didn't have leftover energy to be monitoring the one thing she had taken responsibility for.

After the kids were grown and out of the house, she announced: "I'm not taking care of this house anymore. We need to sell it. We'll buy a condo and save the rest."

The money from the house sale went into a joint bank account. Shortly after they were in the new condo, she took all the money from the account and announced that she was leaving him. Over the years, not only had she maneuvered ownership of the known investments, she had siphoned off large sums of money that he was never able to trace.

> A girlfriend may camouflage stealing from her boyfriend by "borrowing" money without any intention of ever paying it back.

Stealing

A woman might steal her partner's money or things on a first date, during a relationship, as she's going out the door at the relationship's end, or even after a breakup.

It seems that, in many jurisdictions, one marriage partner taking community property funds without the spouse's knowledge is not viewed as stealing. The money is considered to belong to both of them and each of them. The same appears true of any money put into joint bank accounts held by partners who are not officially married.

In a dating or living-together relationship, a woman might take her partner's money or things without his knowledge, or she might camouflage stealing funds by "borrowing" money from him with no intention of ever paying it back.

A man who ends up holding the empty bag of unrepaid "loans" to an ex may get down on himself for ever trusting her, but chances are she did a great sales job convincing him on both her need for the money and her intention to repay him when something changed for her.

A malicious woman may initially build up her partner's confidence that she will pay back anything he lends her by asking for small loans which she does pay back, but it's just part of a bigger con to get more out of him.

If the loans aren't documented, she can claim that he gifted the money to her and he would have little legal recourse. Even if the loans are documented, and he secures a judgment against her for the loaned amount, in many cases, it is difficult to impossible to actually obtain repayment.

Once a married couple separates physically, their incomes also typically separate and become their own property. From that same point, debt incurred by one is typically considered that individual's debt.

A man worked two jobs at a time for most of his marriage trying to support himself and his wife. She worked one job at minimal pay but spent lavishly on herself. She was controlling, demanding, demeaning, and unfaithful. Eventually, they separated.

Six months after they separated, the estranged wife was crying that she was having money problems. She was unable to get a credit card because of her bad credit and she had no money for emergencies. The man felt sorry for her (he was conditioned for years to feel sorry for her), so he agreed to add her name to his credit card. She promised she would reimburse him if she ever *had* to use the card.

That was her promise. That's not what happened.

She used his credit card to get concert tickets for her friends, prepay hundreds of dollars for a personal trainer, and buy a very expensive designer purse. She couldn't afford any of these things, and neither could he.

The estranged wife didn't pay any of the credit card debt. Time and again, she reassured him that she would pay him for anything she charged, but she never paid for any of it.

Finally, he woke up to the reality of the situation and told her she couldn't use the card anymore. He had her name taken off the account. What did she do? She tried to use the card again and called her ex complaining, "Why doesn't the card work?"

Ruining his credit

An abusive woman may ruin her partner's credit by way of overspending, or she may set out with the intent to damage his credit to punish him for perceived "wrongs" or just for sport.

> "Your financial life may still be intertwined with your ex-wife's, even long after the marriage is over."
> —Kimberly Palmer,
> *US News & World Report*

An intimate relationship offers access to personal information such as social security numbers. After a breakup, a woman may take advantage of that access, steal her former partner's identity, and use it to get credit cards or loans. If she doesn't make the payments, his credit can take a hit.

A man owned a home before his girlfriend moved in. When she became his wife and refinancing the house seemed to make sense, the title and mortgage were put in both their names. They were married little more than a year before they separated. She got to stay in the house.

During the year that it took to get a divorce settlement completed and filed, she repeatedly paid the mortgage late on purpose to damage his credit rating. He knew she had the money to make the payments, but she made each payment just in time to prevent foreclosure while late enough to impact his credit score.

When he went to rent a place for himself, he had to pay $250 for the past-due electric bill on the house she was occupying before he was allowed to open another account for his rental. Again, she had the money to pay her bills, she just chose not to, and it reflected negatively on his credit-worthiness.

Keeping the family financially burdened

One partner keeping the family financially burdened may have the intended effect of limiting the other partner's ability to escape the relationship. In some relationships, the tethering may be a less-intentional side effect of a partner's selfish overspending or under-contributing.

Men who are scurrying trying to keep ahead of bills and debt may not have time or energy left over to contemplate their personal situation. Life is passing them by at such high speed that their vision is blurred.

A partner can use this condition to her advantage if she wants to keep her man tied to her. If she racks up debt and coerces him to spend more than he can afford, he may be running so fast to meet the financial obligations that he can't see anything else.

This is not unlike the unethical business ploy to keep employees attached to their jobs by encouraging them to go into debt and overcommit themselves financially. In the days of the company store, workers became indebted to their bosses as they racked up a line of credit buying groceries. They couldn't move on without paying the debt, and they often couldn't pay the debt, so they were stuck with their job no matter what the conditions or demands.

Even if a man being used in this way by his partner does get clarity and realize that she is unreasonable with dollars and sense, he may feel too broke to leave the relationship. The unfeasibility of sustaining the cost of a breakup, and supporting a household for himself (and potentially one for her as well), may cause him to redirect his mind if any thoughts of leaving should happen to pop up.

Refusing to contribute financially

A woman may refuse to contribute financially to the household by:

- being intentionally underemployed,
- not being employed at all,
- pretending she can't work, or
- insisting that any money she makes is hers alone.

A woman may insist that her income is hers, and his income is the family's. This is an old idea with roots in an era when bored middle-class women sometimes worked part-time for a little pocket money. It was an era when women didn't have many options or opportunity for well-paid work. This unequal idea should have disappeared along with the equality gains of the women's movement.

A man's wife was employed before and after they were married, but stopped employment with the birth of their child. He agreed that it made sense for her to focus on raising their son until he was old enough for school.

The agreed-upon time for her return to employment came and went. The wife had one excuse, after another, after another why she couldn't get a job. The man felt used and discouraged as she went to lunches with friends and he toiled away at his job.

In an effort to support her doing something income-producing that she seemed enthusiastic about, the man agreed to purchase materials for a business venture his wife discovered. After the materials were purchased, she seemed focused on building the business. The man eventually discovered that his wife had become discouraged about the business, had abandoned it completely, and was just putting up the facade of working.

While a woman might abuse her partner by refusing to contribute equally during their relationship, men are particularly vulnerable to this abuse during and after divorce.

If a man presents himself in divorce court as being unemployed or underemployed, the judge is likely to be all over him with instructions to clean up his act. If a woman presents herself as unemployed or underemployed, the judge is much more likely to get the man she is divorcing to support her. She may have to come up with some excuses for her lack of income, but manipulative women are good at that sort of thing.

Many, many a man has been tethered to his perfectly capable ex-wife by support orders he can't afford. (This is *not* to take anything away from sound support orders which are based on reality and not distortion. Nor is it meant to discount the fact that there are times when men avoid paying support that they should legitimately be paying.)

> A book (that shall remain nameless) whose purpose is to teach women how to take advantage of their husband during divorce tells its readers to be unemployed as long as possible before filing for divorce and lists ideas on how to create a cover story for not being able to work.

A divorcing woman may put herself in the best position possible for support by feigning illness. She may doctor-shop to find one who will back up her desired diagnosis, lie about the existence of symptoms, or even go so far as to create symptoms on purpose.

Limiting his ability to work

A woman may limit her partner's ability to work in order to control him. She may discourage schooling or training that would better his position. She may fear that education would take too much time and attention away from her or make him superior to her in some way.

She may sabotage his job as punishment for ending their relationship or just because she enjoys destroying people. She may contact his boss or co-workers with demeaning or undermining stories. Or, she may achieve her abusive goals by threatening to do any of the above.

She may get in the way of his job by demanding that he not be away from her much because of her jealousy or neediness. Or, she may distract him at work with incessant texting, becoming angry if he doesn't respond.

A man who had married his wife after he had a well-established career and strong savings was on the brink of separation. He had endured severe emotional and physical abuse from his wife but was hopeful that they could be happy together. In a last-ditch effort to save the marriage, he agreed to go to couples counseling.

The counselor had them each make a list of what they wanted from their partner. The wife's list was short. She wanted her husband to shut down his medical practice so that he would have more time to devote to her, and replace their pre-nuptial agreement with a post-nuptial agreement more favorable to her.

Her blatant attempt to coerce him into turning his back on the career that he loved and opening up his life savings to her gave him the clarity he needed to let the marriage go.

Destroying his property

Sometimes an abusive woman will destroy her partner's possessions as an act of control or jealousy. This was the case when a woman deleted all the pictures her husband had that predated their relationship.

More commonly, a woman will destroy her partner's possessions because she is punishing him. It seems like any woman who decides she has been "scorned," or whose love for her man has turned to hatred, is given free rein to destroy his stuff.

A woman angry that her boyfriend had ended their relationship set his car on fire.

A man came home from a business trip to find every piece of his clothing, from suits to socks, cut up by his wife. She erroneously thought he was having an affair.

Between a couple's separation and divorce, the house trailer that had been the husband's before the marriage sat on their joint property. He was denied access to the property and trailer during the separation, but was awarded the trailer in the divorce.

When the man went to pick up his trailer, he realized that his ex had purposefully broken the roof vents to expose the interior to the elements. Rain had been coming in for a whole year. The trailer was destroyed.

Every item this man had not taken with him when he initially fled the house was partially ruined by his ex before he was able to retrieve it: "My son's game box had the joystick and the box, but the program was wrecked. She deleted all my pictures from my computer . . ."

Physical abuse

"My ex-wife would grab me, scratch my face, tear my shirt.
If I tried to get away,
she'd stand in the doorway and block the exit.
She'd take my car keys.
Sometimes, she would park her car behind mine
or drive my car away so I couldn't escape.
I never got physical back. I kept hoping she'd stop."

Overview

Physical abuse of a partner is the category of abuse that gets the most attention. When I became aware of abuse of men by women, I wasn't expecting to see or hear much about physical abuse, but I have been surprised by how many examples of physical abuse by women I have encountered.

Many studies that address domestic violence statistics treat it like a competition. Do more women get attacked by their partners than men get attacked by partners? What's their relative injury and death count?

There are different answers to these questions depending on the research methods used and the inclinations of researchers, and yet, the undeniable bottom line is that many men are being physically abused by female partners and it is debilitating and dangerous to the men, their children, and the women who are acting out in this way.

To declare physical abuse of men by women as unworthy of attention or concern because some researchers say that more women than men sustain severe or lethal injury from their partners is like promoting ignoring brain cancer because it doesn't occur as often or kill as many people as lung cancer. (The American Cancer Society's numbers show lung/bronchus cancers to be ten times the rate of brain/nervous system cancers both by incidence and deaths, but people aren't clamoring for brain cancer to be ignored.)

> Women can overcome their strength disadvantage in many ways.

Men's size and strength advantage over women has been among deciding factors that have led many people to conclude that physical abuse of a man by a woman is a non-issue.

However, women who physically abuse men can overcome their strength disadvantage in many ways, including:

- surprise attacks,
- the use of objects either as direct weapons or projectiles,
- striking when their prey is in a vulnerable position (driving, asleep, drunk, has his back turned . . .),
- counting on their partner to not strike back, or
- soliciting the help of others to attack him.

A man may prevent himself from striking back because of training or desire to not hurt a woman, his non-violent nature, or concern that he will get in legal trouble. Even when his partner is whaling on him, a man may restrain himself from countering the attack.

Women use a variety of methods to physically abuse their partners:

- throwing or breaking things
- scratching
- kicking
- biting
- hair-pulling
- burning
- shoving
- interfering with sleeping or eating
- blocking exits
- poisoning
- hitting with open hands or fists
- hitting with objects
- forcing him out of the house
- attacking, or threatening to attack, others
- assaulting with knives, guns, or vehicles

Throwing or breaking things

An abusive woman may attack her partner with an object directly, or throw things at, near, or away from him.

If a thrown object doesn't inflict physical pain on her partner, it still achieves abusive objectives:

- It gives her the high and relief that comes with the angry outburst.
- It may break the thrown object, thereby destroying something of importance to her partner.
- It is a threatening gesture that puts him in the position of having to capitulate or risk escalation of abuse.

Throwing an object at her partner puts both the weight and velocity of the object into the equation, and gives her the advantage of distance, limiting his ability to retaliate.

The diet soda commercial described in Chapter 1 made light of a woman throwing a can of soda at her husband, but it's really not a laughing matter. I have heard stories of men who have required stitches to repair cuts sustained from being hit in the head by soda cans thrown by their wife or girlfriend.

Throwing an object near a partner is equivalent to a warning shot: change or else it will be very bad for you. And a question remains. Was it a purposeful miss or an intended direct hit that missed the mark? The not knowing adds to the intimidation.

> Throwing an object near a partner is the equivalent of a warning shot: change or else it will be very bad for you.

Throwing an object away from a partner gets the change-or-else point across while protecting the thrower and partner from the aftermath of a direct hit. It may allow the woman to justify her actions because, after all, she doesn't throw things *at* people. That is, as long as no broken parts fly towards anyone, and no one—such as a child—inadvertently enters the projectile's path.

A woman became angry when she was arguing with her husband in the kitchen. She picked up a cup and threw it. She didn't throw it at him, but it was still a dangerous and threatening choice. She didn't recognize it as abusive until someone else labeled it as such. The discussion motivated her to stop that type of behavior and focus on improving her communication skills instead.

A man's wife threw "whatever she could get her hands on" when she was mad. One time, she threw a laptop. "Keys were a common projectile." She often grabbed his keys as he was about to get into the car and threw them on the ground, breaking many key chains. The key chains were sentimental to him because he had purchased the original the first month they were together. Each time she broke it, he would buy a replacement.

Another man's story: "The afternoon of our wedding, she began morphing into her true personality: demanding, rageful, and self-centered. If I ever said no to her, things would get broken. I'd be talking to her on the phone. She'd be eating cereal. Something would set her off and I could hear the cereal bowl hit the wall. She'd cry and apologize saying she was going through a lot. She'd act nice for a while. I kept thinking we could fix things."

Cat-fighting techniques

A Google search for kicking, biting, and scratching pointed towards articles about the challenges of dealing with domestic and wild cats, big and small. Women are known to use all of these, along with hair-pulling, when fighting each other. They also use these techniques to attack men.

Men are particularly vulnerable to being kicked in the groin, and an abusive woman may capitalize on this vulnerability.

> Cat-fighting techniques women use on men:
>
> kicking
> biting
> scratching
> hair-pulling

A well-educated middle-aged man, now happily remarried, described abuses he endured during his previous marriage, including that his angry ex would jump on his back and scratch at his face.

Another man was married for twenty years to a beautiful professional woman who flew into rages over whatever thing she decided he had done wrong that day. Her fits often included scratching his face and grabbing at the clothes he was wearing, often tearing his shirt.

Some biting attacks by women are so extreme that they result in severed body parts.

Incensed by the possibility of her marriage ending, Ameryst Blaylock punched her husband in the face, jumped on top of him, and bit half of his lower lip off. During the attack she announced "If you don't want *me*, I'm going to make sure no one wants *you*."[1]

Burning

An abusive woman may burn her partner by:

- throwing hot coffee at him,
- pouring boiling water on him,
- burning him with cigarettes,
- attacking him with a hot iron,
- spraying him with bleach or other chemicals,
- poking him with hot fireplace tools, or
- setting the bed on fire while he is sleeping.

British businessman Ian McNicholl is alive today because a neighbor called the police in 2008 and triggered his rescue from two years of violent abuse from his girlfriend, Michelle Williamson. Before the police arrived, he had endured many sustained hours of physical attack.

The relationship had started out well. Michelle didn't begin hitting Ian with her fist and objects until they had been living together for several months. By then, she was working on isolating him from his friends and family. She blocked Ian from fleeing the relationship by threatening that her brothers would kill him if he abandoned her.

On one occasion, she burned him on several parts of his body with an iron. On still another, she poured boiling water onto his lap. Other times, she put lit cigarettes up his nose, pressed the lit ends of cigarettes into his chest, and sprayed his eyes with bleach. Each time she hurt him, her threats of retribution kept him from seeking medical care.

Scars all over his body supplied an abundance of evidence for the trial which followed his rescue and resulted in Michelle being sentenced to seven years in prison.

Shoving

Shoving is not simply touching someone in a way that sends the message "stop." It implies the use of force to aggressively move someone. The person who is shoved will typically fall back from the impact or be pushed into something (walls, furniture . . .). They may be physically hurt by the impact of falling or hitting the object they are pushed into.

The verb *shove* is defined as to:

- push something with force (Merriam-Webster.com)
- push someone or something roughly (OxfordDictionaries.com)

My parents argued with each other a lot. Slapping and hitting us kids was pretty common, but I only saw them get physical with each other once.

I was about twelve years old. Dad was definitely drunk at the time, and Mom may or may not have been sober. They were arguing and Mom pushed Dad into the sewing machine. This was *not* a defensive action by Mom; this was definitely her escalating the situation.

Dad landed on the swing-out sewing machine tabletop, bending the metal arm whose job it was to support the tabletop in the open position while using the machine. It was a shocking and scary thing to witness. I worried about how far this heightened fighting was going to go, but Dad didn't retaliate and things eventually settled down.

The crooked positioning of the sewing machine cabinet top was a forever-more reminder to me of that day.

Interfering with sleeping or eating

The popular saying "never go to bed mad" is flawed advice. It can drive arguments way too far into the night, until brains aren't functioning very well. A person being forced to keep talking or face the wrath of their partner can be not only in mental and emotional stress but also physical pain from need for sleep.

Deprivation of food and sleep are well-known torture techniques. They are included in what is commonly called *Biderman's Chart of Coercion.* (See page 134 for more about the chart.) Biderman places "semi-starvation" and "sleep deprivation" in the "Induced Debilitation, Exhaustion" category. He describes the effect/purpose as "weakens mental and physical ability to resist."[2]

While the degree to which sleeping and eating are deprived in partner abuse would not likely be as severe as that experienced by the POWs Biderman studied, there still is a negative impact. The negative impact may be not only the immediate pain and stress of exhaustion, but there may also be longer-term effects of sleep deprivation.

Sleep deprivation can reduce a man's capacity to think clearly in the days that follow the sleep deprivation, interfering with his ability to cope and diminishing his performance at work and in life in general. That may have repercussions for his health, career, and relationships.

A man who had a dangerous job was often kept up most of the night by his angry wife. His family worried that the lack of sleep made it difficult for him to have the mental alertness and responsiveness to be safe at work. Their worst fears were realized when he had an accident at work after a couple of sleepless nights—and died from his injuries.

Blocking exits

Interfering with someone's ability to exit controls their whereabouts and keeps the person within the abuser's physical and psychological reach. It steals a partner's ability to protect himself from pummeling or badgering.

Salespeople know that if their perspective buyer leaves the premises or ends a conversation without agreeing to buy, they are much less likely to make a sale. Statistically, giving them time to think about the purchase doesn't pay off for the seller.

Leaving an abusive situation may give the target of abuse the chance to clear his head and see the reality of the situation or formulate an argument so he can present his perspective on a topic. An abusive partner may not want that.

> An abusive person may not want the target of their abuse to get away from their influence or reach.

An abusive woman might block her partner's exit from:

- a room,
- an area, or
- their home.

A man's wife often became demeaning, argumentative, and physically abusive. When he would try to leave, she would stand in the doorway, sometimes grabbing his arms to stop him. She further contained him by hiding his car keys or parking her or a friend's car behind his. She would sometimes drive his car away (leaving him with no transportation, as she always retained control of the keys to her car).

Poisoning

Women are often in an ideal position to poison their husband or boyfriend if they happen to be inclined to do so. A quick online search came up with many news accounts of confirmed partner-poisonings by women. Here are a few of those stories:

A Pennsylvania man's repeated illnesses over a span of three years stimulated doctors to perform tests that uncovered an unusual chemical in his blood. Police discovered that the man's girlfriend, Vickie Jo Mills, had been lacing his drinking water with Visine eye drops. Vickie Jo explained that she put the drops in her boyfriend's water on ten occasions to get his attention.

September 2013: Tianle Li, a New Jersey woman, was convicted of killing her husband, Ming Wang, by poisoning him several times with odorless, tasteless thallium. She obtained the extremely potent poison through her job as a chemist at a large pharmaceutical company.

Ming had moved out of their home and filed for divorce, but his wife convinced him to move back in to help take care of their toddler son. A few months later, on the day the divorce was to be final, Ming admitted himself to the hospital for abdominal pain. It appears that Tianle continued to poison her husband in the hospital while she presented herself as a caring, doting wife.

Another case involved antifreeze. Several months after Delaware resident James Baker died suddenly, investigators followed the trail of evidence back to his home. In March 2014, his wife, Jamie, confessed to spiking her husband's steroids by injecting the bottles with antifreeze.

Hitting with open hands and fists

We train males to "don't hit girls" while we teach women that it's their right to slap a man if they're mad at him. A woman hauling off and slapping a man is viewed as deserved. She deserves to do it and he must have deserved to get it. He's supposed to stand there and take it and not retaliate.

A man slapping a woman is physical abuse. And a woman slapping a man is physical abuse. The intention of the slap, regardless of whether it has the force to blacken an eye or break a jaw, is to control, demean, or punish: that's abusive.

Men who are physically abused may also have their partner pound on them with their closed fists. Women often get away with this despite strength and size differentials because their partner is:

- non-violent,
- unwilling to hit a woman, or
- afraid of what might happen if he hits her back.

A man may fear striking back because of concern that his strength might result in her being hurt, or concern that she is trying to draw fire so she can accuse him of domestic violence and call the police.

A man's wife often violently hammered him with her fists, pounding him all over his body. At times, she would encourage their teenage sons to beat him as well. He would curl up to try and protect himself from the blows, but he didn't physically fight back. He was not a physically violent person. He hoped that reasoning with his wife would make the attacks stop.

Hitting with objects

Women get more bang for their buck (an ironic play on words if you think of *buck* as a term for a male deer) by using the weight of an object to assist them to inflict harm. The object could be a bat, golf club, or anything handy.

A man I mentioned in Chapter 1, *Women abuse men? Does that happen?*, was woken up in the middle of the night by his wife pounding him with the clock radio. She hit him in both arms, the chest, and face—right beside his eye—before he fled the house and called the police.

They hadn't argued that day. The attack came out of nowhere. He had become accustomed to her being controlling, demanding, and manipulating, even throwing things, but she had never hit him before.

He was cut and bruised from the attack, which upon further reflection seemed to be an attempt on her part to provoke him to fight back so she could get him into legal trouble. He hadn't known beforehand, but she seemed to have been trying to put herself in the best position to divorce him.

On Valentine's Day 2010, a woman and her sister walked into a restaurant and violently attacked the woman's ex-boyfriend with her spike-heeled shoes, cutting his face. "He tried to ignore them, police reported, even as they began hitting him."[3]

A different man didn't survive the beating he received by a girlfriend wielding high heels. In April 2014, Ana Trujillo was found guilty of killing her boyfriend, university professor Alf Andersson, by hitting him over twenty times in the face, neck, and head with her platform high-heel shoe. At the trial, Ana's defense was . . . (can you guess?)

. . . it was his fault. She claimed it was self-defense.

Prosecutors pointed out that Ana had no defensive wounds but Alf had defensive wounds on his wrists and hands.

"Prosecutors told jurors that after a night of drinking, the couple began arguing and during the confrontation, Andersson was injured and fell on his back. Trujillo sat on Andersson, preventing him from getting up and repeatedly struck him in the face and head with her shoe, they said."[4]

During the trial, two other men testified that she had been physically violent with each of them when they were dating.

Alf Andersson's murder had so many of the classic elements found in abuse of men by women:

- He was rendered less able to defend himself by intoxication and falling on his back.
- She used an object to increase her ability to cause harm.
- She blamed him for her having to hurt him.
- He had even paid for the $1,500 shoes she used to kill him.

A woman who was demanding and controlling, lied, had affairs, emptied joint bank accounts . . . and generally terrorized her husband, physically abused him in a way that defies categorization: she put needles into his favorite dessert. When he discovered the needles, she acted like it was a joke.

> A woman who *distorts the truth to get a restraining order* so she can force her partner out of his home is abusing her partner and the system meant to protect people who actually need the protection.

Forcing him out of the house

Men may be forced out of the homes they share with their partners through pressure or by court order.

A woman who gets a restraining order against her partner to secure the home for herself and her children when she is legitimately frightened for her and their safety is making a healthy choice. A woman who *distorts the truth to get a restraining order* against her partner to force him out of the home so she can punish, control, or demean him is abusive.

The man whose wife hit him with the clock radio (I referred to him in Chapter 1 and the previous section) fled the house and called the police.

Somehow, his wife was able to get charges against her changed from domestic violence to simple assault. She spent a few days in jail.

The day she was released, the man came home to find her in a rage, throwing his clothes and personal items into the front yard. He called the police. The police officer suggested that he take the things that were in the yard and work the rest of it out in court.

She filed for a protection order. Even though she was the one that was violent and he had never hit or threatened her, she secured the protection order against him. The order denied him access to the house (which had been his before their short marriage) and all of his remaining belongings.

Attacking, or threatening to attack, others

One way to secure compliance to your demands is to attack, or threaten to attack, someone or something the target of your demands loves. The mob does it. Gangs do it. And some abusive women do it.

A vivid example is portrayed in the bloody horse head scene in *The Godfather*. Don Corleone lets a movie mogul know that he wants him to have a Corleone family friend star in a movie. The mogul refuses. The next morning, he wakes up with the severed head of his beloved horse in his bed beside him. The murder of the horse is both a suffered negative consequence of the mogul's assertiveness and a threat that there would be more severe retribution if he doesn't comply with the Don's wishes. He complies.

An abusive woman may attack, or threaten to attack, her partner's:

- children,
- pets,
- family or friends,
- prized possessions, or
- anything that he cares about.

A couple was working on reconciling after the wife had an affair. When the husband tried to express his hurt and concerns, his wife would act despondent and threaten to hurt herself and the kids. The husband didn't know what to think. Were they idle threats or a real possibility?

The focus totally switched away from recognition of the damage done to him by her affair to caretaking his wife and trying to figure out what he needed to do to keep everyone safe.

Assaulting with vehicles

Using a car as a weapon is one of the many ways for a woman to nullify any size or strength difference between her and the target of her abuse.

An angry abusive woman may:

- drive recklessly while her partner is a passenger in the car to instill fear or punish him for something she feels he has done wrong,
- take control of the car when he is driving, or
- use a vehicle to run him down.

A woman was driving on the highway with her husband when they found themselves suddenly being chased by his ex-wife. The enraged ex-wife eventually ran them off the road. Luckily they were not physically injured, but the incident contributed to their decision to move far away to get out of her reach.

In another case, an enraged woman took control of the steering wheel while her husband was driving. She shot the car off the road into a ditch, creating extreme danger not only for herself and her husband, but also for their young children who were in the back seat.

Another man was at his home trying to move out his belongings. He was splitting from his wife who had a history of violence against him. He was trying to get his things before she came home. She arrived as he was in the driveway with a box in his arms. Enraged, she drove straight towards him, pinning him between his car and hers. Both of his legs were broken by the impact.

Assaulting with knives and guns

The 2013 televised murder trial of Jodi Arias helped draw attention in the US to the issue of women attacking their male partners with knives and guns.

For Jodi, using a knife *or* a gun to attack her ex-boyfriend, Travis Alexander, wasn't enough. Jodi used both a knife *and* a gun to attack Travis. She stabbed him twenty-seven times, slit his throat, and shot him in the head.

A man who lived in my area, Randy Ferguson, was shot in the head twice by his wife while their young daughter looked on. Then his wife solicited the help of her adult children (Randy's step-children) to dispose of his body and clean up the murder scene. They stuffed his body in the trunk of his car and proceeded to move the car around for the next several days, trying to elude police detection. A week after Randy went missing, his car and body were found just a few miles from my home.

Physically abusive women often threaten, or attack, their partners with knives. For every knifing that ends in murder and makes it into the headlines, there are many, many more attacks that are hidden from the public.

Michelle Mills murdered her boyfriend, Eddie Miller, by stabbing him twenty-four times in his back, chest, and stomach. This was not the first time Michelle had used knife attacks on her partners: "during a four-week trial . . . two former boyfriends testified that Michelle had attacked them with knives. Charges had never been brought against her."[5]

Soliciting the help of others to attack him

Friends, relatives, new partners, or acquaintances may be used by a manipulative woman to extend her abusive reach. As evidenced by the story of Randy Ferguson's murder mentioned in the previous section, a violently abusive woman may even use her children to aid in her attacks.

A woman bent on getting rid of her male partner can overcome her size disadvantage and simultaneously cover her tracks by getting another man to do her dirty work. This is sometimes achieved by contracting with him for financial reward, other times by manipulating and/or seducing him.

Karen Lofren is a pretty middle-aged woman who lived in my small community, worked as a pediatric nurse at the local hospital, and was caught hiring someone to kill her estranged husband. Luckily for her estranged husband, the guy she hired to kill him was an undercover detective.

Karen offered the "hit man" half of the million-dollar life insurance policy she had on her husband. She told him to make it look like a botched robbery and gave him diamond earrings as a down payment for the murder. She supplied a photo of her husband and details of his schedule.

While the recordings of her meetings with the undercover officer and other evidence created an open-and-shut case, Karen asked for leniency in sentencing, blaming an unnamed person for putting the idea of the murder in her head, and offering an apology for her "error in judgment." Her defense asked for probation, citing only that this was her first criminal act. Fifty people wrote letters saying how wonderful Karen is. Luckily, in this case, the judge wasn't swayed. Karen received a sentence at the high end of the standard range: 13.75 years.

Chapter 8

Spiritual abuse

"Body wounds heal and scar;
a wounded soul requires support and a lifetime to heal."

Overview

Spiritual and religious beliefs and practices go to the core of who you are. When they are used as a weapon against you, the wounding can be extremely deep and devastating. Being abused in this way can create spiritual turmoil and discombobulate your view of the world.

Spiritual abuse is the use of religious or spiritual practices, beliefs, organizations, leaders, or communities to abuse another human being.

Spiritual abuse of a partner involves distortion, extortion, or extraction. The abusive person:

- *distorts* spiritual or religious beliefs and practices so that they can be used to control, demean, or punish;
- uses spiritual beliefs, communities, or leaders to *extort* compliance through force or threats; or
- uses the communities or leaders to *extract* punishment for attempting to defy her abuses or *extracts* him from his religious community.

Examples of ways a woman may spiritually abuse her male partner include:

- using religious or spiritual practices, beliefs, or organizations to abuse or justify abuse;
- enlisting religious administration to coerce acceptance of abuse;
- interfering with performance of reasonable spiritual practices and connection with religious community;
- ridiculing his beliefs; or
- forcing him to participate in religious practices.

Using religion to abuse

An abusive woman may use her partner's religious beliefs or community as a mechanism for abuse.

She may use scripture to justify her behavior and compliance with her controlling demands or to keep the target of abuse entrapped.

She may use her partner's spiritual aspirations as a means of attack, throwing scripture at him: bombing him with accusations that he isn't complying with the spiritual values that he holds dear.

Religious attachment to the sanctity of marriage can cause an abused person to stay no matter what. An abusive woman can potentially use her partner's desire to honor his marriage commitment to her advantage, keeping him locked in marriage regardless of how badly she treats him.

Members of religious or spiritual communities may be manipulated into becoming accomplices in abuse. They can be engaged to control a woman's partner by pressuring him to do as she wishes, become further sources of demeaning or belittling feedback, or exert punishment by shunning.

> A community that a man cherished as a nurturing haven may turn painfully unwelcoming. The loss can pile betrayal and rejection on top of other breakup challenges.

Rumors can spread like wildfire in religious communities. When a man ends a relationship, a vindictive woman may find many willing ears for her stories of how her man done her wrong, whether or not those stories are true.

Enlisting religious leaders to coerce

We usually look up to our ministers, priests, and spiritual leaders. We can be greatly influenced by their opinion, possibly even convinced that they speak for God and confident that their guidance is the means of spiritual and everlasting health.

> Spiritual leaders may willingly or unwittingly become part of an abusive woman's schemes to control, demean, or punish her partner.

It can be shocking and devastating if those people who you thought had your best interests at heart turn out to demand your compliance with unreasonable conditions, either because of their inability to see the reality of the situation or because the religion itself is abusive.

Religious leaders are often not familiar with the abuse of men by women and may not be well equipped to protect themselves from becoming part of an abusive woman's schemes to control, demean, or punish her partner.

An abused man may feel as if he is forced to choose between his religion—which he has relied on for guidance, inspiration, and support—and his (and his children's) mental, physical, financial, and possibly even spiritual, well-being. It's a disturbing choice to have to make.

A minister of a moderate Christian church, who I knew had counseled many people over many years, had a very adamant response when I mentioned that one of my specialties is the abuse *of* men *by* women. He said: "That doesn't happen in this area." I know for sure that he was wrong, and I am equally confident that his blindness could open him up to unwittingly being used by a female parishioner to further entrap her partner.

A woman who was a member of another religious community had been emotionally abusive to her husband for many years. After he asked for a divorce and moved out of their home, she stalked and harassed him.

She went to their church elders and harassed them with her many distorted stories of his wrongdoing and insistence that they step in. Worn out, they capitulated and called the estranged husband in for a meeting. They told him to do whatever she asked of him. They were not interested in his side of the story. He was shocked and dismayed.

> Spiritual abuse can create a crisis of faith and traumatic disillusionment.

This first calling onto the carpet by the elders was devastating in and of itself, but unfortunately it was just the beginning of the woman's use of their religious leaders as an extension of her abusive reach. Eventually, they threatened him with excommunication.

Through much inner turmoil and excruciatingly painful reexamination of his understanding of the religion that had been the center of his life for many years, he took the arduous step of removing himself as a member.

Interference

A woman may abuse her partner by interfering with his performance of spiritual or religious practices. Getting in the way of a partner's participation in his religion isolates him from his support group, both in the physical realm and the spiritual realm.

A man had a strong attachment to his church since his childhood. When he was dating the woman who would become his wife, she was very supportive of his regular attendance at church. As soon as the couple married, the wife began her stealth isolation campaign, which included separating him from his church community.

She waged a two-pronged campaign: interfere with his ability to attend church, and interfere with his relationship with other parishioners.

She subtly undermined his ability to attend church by making him seem like he was being unkind if he chose to go to services. She went out of her way to schedule events on Saturday nights and keep the kids out late.

Sunday morning, both she and the kids would complain about how tired they were. She'd say: "Let's not get up and go to church today." If he chose church, he would feel like he was being pushy and unreasonable. If he said he would go alone, he would feel like he was abandoning her and not being considerate.

She told him stories about bad things that church members said about her and him. He didn't realize at the time that her stories were lies. She was successful in making him feel rejected and betrayed by the church. He detached himself from church events, members, and religion entirely.

Ridiculing and Forcing

If someone wants to really hurt another person, then ridiculing that which defines him is a very effective way to achieve her goal. Spiritual beliefs and practices are very important to many people and an integral part of who they are. Unfortunately, that can make them a susceptible target for demeaning comments and attitudes.

Having discussions about differing spiritual views can be part of a healthy relationship. Shaming or belittling a partner for his spiritual beliefs and practices is abusive.

Treating a partner's items of spiritual significance with disdain and disrespect sends a message of deep disdain and disrespect for the partner.

Forcing a partner to participate in religious services and practices that he finds abhorrent is also abusive. The forcing may be via threat, intimidation, or there being a price to pay for non-compliance.

> As one abused man put it: "An attack made on someone's spirituality is the lowest and the most villainous of the blows. If a woman manages to concuss, or worse yet, destroy her partner's spirituality, she has taken complete control of that poor individual."

An abusive woman may push or entice her partner into going against his religious beliefs and standards. Manipulating a partner to not adhere to his religious beliefs can have a devastating impact. It can create agonizing inner conflict.

Any of the manipulation methods listed in Chapter 10, page 126, can be used by a woman to exert force on a partner to bend to her will rather than follow his conscience.

Legal abuse

"Even though I had never been at all abusive
or threatening to my wife (or anyone else),
she lied and said she was scared of me
so she could get a restraining order against me.
That meant I couldn't go back to the house for
my tools, or documents, or anything."

Overview

A woman's use of the legal or judicial system to control, demean, or punish her partner or ex-partner is legal abuse. In these cases, police officers, lawyers, judges, domestic violence advocates, and the justice system itself become her accomplices. Unfortunately, such individuals and systems cooperate with women's abuses far too often. (I'm *not* saying that they are *always* skewed in favor of women, just that it is happening a lot.)

There was a time when North American women had few rights. A woman's husband could take her children from her and she had no recourse. She could be beaten by her husband and police would not interfere. She was often not believed if she claimed to be the victim of partner abuse.

Times have changed. Unfortunately, rather than graduate to a more just system, far too often, the flip side of these scenarios is happening now: father's relationships with their children are minimized, a man's bruises and wounds are not enough evidence for police protection, and women's statements of "facts" are more heavily weighted than men's.

An abusive woman might falsify information in order to manipulate the legal system so that she can:

- enjoy the benefits of using the domestic violence victim card,
- get an unwarranted restraining/protection order,
- deprive him of access to his children,
- exaggerate her need for child support,
- secure undeserved spousal support, or
- create havoc in his life.

Playing the DV con game

An abusive woman can abuse the advocates and institutions whose goal is protecting people from domestic violence.

Women who cry "abuse" are usually listened to and often believed even in the absence of evidence— even when there is evidence to the contrary.

Attaining victim status can garner a woman:

- sympathy from advocates, police, and judges;
- financial and legal resources through domestic violence agencies; and
- power and control over the man being accused of "abuse" during custody or dissolution battles.

A man suspected his wife was having an affair. He was not the jealous type. They had been together many years and he had never before thought she was cheating on him, but many indicators supported the theory that she was now.

He confronted her with his suspicions and she adamantly denied doing any such thing. He said he believed she was texting another man. She said no, that wasn't true. When he picked up her phone to check it, she started screaming at him: "You put that down or I'll call the police!"

He was shocked. He had never laid a hand on her or threatened her, but he knew that if the police came out she would be very convincing. He was certain that they would believe her, not him. He put the phone down.

Conjuring up a need for protection

A woman can falsify fear in order to get an unnecessary restraining/protection order against her partner. Such maliciously acquired orders are a diabolical way to control, demean, and punish a partner or former partner. An unjustified protection order has far-reaching repercussions to the lives of the men who are "restrained."

Rob Freeman was married for only three years but was under his ex-wife's control for more than a decade after his divorce. Rob's case went to the Washington State Court of Appeals[1] and then on to the state Supreme Court.[2]

It all started with a restraining order Rob's wife secured against him in 1998. Rob was never charged with domestic violence, but his wife was able to obtain a temporary protection order and have that order turned into a permanent protection order. She had used the magic words for getting such an order: she said she was afraid of her husband.

The original order was based on accusations that Rob had once pushed his 16-year-old stepdaughter into her room, while she was in a crouched position, when she had refused to go; and that he had displayed his guns to his wife once. His wife did not accuse Rob of threatening her with the guns. She claimed he had pulled the rifles from their storage case to show her that it was not a hiding spot for jewelry she accused him of stealing from her.

Rob was a Green Beret. He was transferred out of Washington State before his divorce was completed and never returned.

He was deployed to Iraq. During a 2001 military mission, Rob sustained multiple injuries, including the loss of his hand. Because of his injuries, he needed to be retrained for other military positions. This meant that he needed a new security clearance.

But, Rob couldn't get a security clearance because of the permanent protection order held by his ex-wife.

In 2006, Rob moved to terminate the protection order. Rob explained to the court commissioner that by the time of his request, he had not been in contact with his former wife in eight years. He also pointed out that he currently lived in another state halfway across the country, he had never violated any law, and was of no danger to anyone.

His ex-wife fought the removal of the protection order. She claimed she was still afraid of him. As evidence of the need for an ongoing order protecting her, she "pointed to unexplained events that she attributed to Rob, including: rattling of the windows, doors, and walls of her house; repositioning of the driver's seat of her car; receiving Rob's mail at her house; reappearance of missing flower vases; and a hole kicked into her bedroom wall."[3]

Rob's ex admitted to the court that she had never seen Rob do any of the things she accredited to him. The alleged incidents occurred while Rob lived far, far away, and the ex claimed the incidents stopped in January 2003 when she replaced her windows. That meant that all alleged incidents predated Rob's request for modification of the protection order by over three years.

But—she still won. The commissioner ruled that the protection order was to remain in place.

Rob appealed the denial of his request for termination of the protection order. Two years later, the appellate court overruled the lower court's decision. They declared that Rob's ex's "current fear is not reasonable. The denial of the motion to terminate or modify the order is based on untenable reasons and grounds."[4]

But—even that wasn't the end of it. Rob still wasn't free. His ex-wife appealed that decision to the Supreme Court.

In 2010, twelve years after his three-year marriage ended, Rob's lifetime sentence of being under his ex's thumb was finally lifted.

Rob Freeman was finally a free man.

The Supreme Court affirmed the Court of Appeals decision, declaring that, "The commissioner abused her discretion when she denied Rob's motion to terminate the order."[5]

Lest we get too excited that justice prevailed in the end for Rob, I think that it is noteworthy that while the majority of the Washington State Supreme Court justices ruled in favor of Rob being awarded the termination of the protection order, several justices filed a dissention from the majority ruling.

The dissention stated that the Court of Appeals was wrong: the commissioner's denial of Rob's request to terminate the protection order should have been upheld. Three of the four female Supreme Court justices signed the dissention.[6] (The majority ruling was signed by five male justices and one female justice.)

Depriving him of access to his children

A woman may use the legal system to limit or eliminate a father's time with his children, even when he is a good father, even when she doesn't really care that much about the children. She may persuade the court to let her move the children far away from their father or restrict the amount of time he is allowed to see them.

> An abusive woman may distort her parenting to make it appear better than it is, and distort his parenting to make it appear worse than it is.

A mother who is inattentive or even abusive to her children may suddenly turn on the charm and act out the part of super mom with her lawyer, judges, counselors, and child advocates.

She may simultaneously falsely accuse an attentive, caring father of being unavailable, cold, or abusive to her and/or the children.

She may take kernels of truth and expand them into horror stories:

- His innocent tickling of his daughter is recounted with the inference that the "tickling" was sexually motivated.
- His healthy requirement that his children do their homework gets turned into obsessive demands.

Cultural bias in favor of women and mothers makes it relatively easy to convince all levels of child welfare decision-makers that her presentation of "facts" is true.

Distorting her need for financial support

A manipulative woman may be willing to say and do anything to get a court to make a man pay dearly for ever having been involved with her, and carry her far beyond their relationship years. There are several potential vehicles for getting her former partner to pay: division of assets, child support, and spousal support.

Common methods for maximizing her breakup payday:

- exaggerating the financial picture that existed during the partnership,
- downplaying her own contribution during the partnership while overstating the man's,
- inflating his current and future expected income,
- understating her own income-producing ability, or
- quitting her job.

A man's estranged wife claimed to the court that she had PTSD from being abused by him while they were married.

He had not been abusive. The opposite was true. She had been abusive to him during and after the marriage. She claimed she was unable to work because of her "PTSD."

The man and his lawyer put up a valiant fight to expose the wife's lies, but the court awarded the perfectly capable wife long-term spousal support that he could not afford.

The court effectively rendered the man an indentured servant to the woman who had abused him.

Creating havoc in his life

> A woman who is willing to lie to the court expends a few minutes creating the lie, but it takes untold hours for her divorcing partner to prove the lie wrong.

Malicious women will use the legal system to create stress and turmoil for partners that dare break free. Even when it's the woman herself that instigates a breakup, she may choose to use the legal system to toy with her ex.

A bad divorce is time consuming, mentally exhausting, and emotionally draining. Each time a man has to meet with his lawyer, prepare a declaration, find a document, or attend a court hearing takes time and energy that is not then available for working or living a normal life. Each time his lawyer has to contact her lawyer, create a document, prepare for court, or attend court, it adds to his bill.

During a divorce, an abusive woman may:

- create frivolous lists of Interrogatories and Requests for Production;
- not respond to his lawyer's requests for information and paperwork, requiring repeated appeals for the discovery materials, and even contempt hearings;
- fight for absurd and unreasonable division of assets;
- thwart his attempts to negotiate;
- go out of her way to be uncooperative so that he has to try multiple times to get even simple settlement tasks completed;
- use a protection order to keep him away from his possessions and documents, requiring that he get court orders or give up his belongings; and/or
- use the children as pawns.

Chapter 10

Emotional/psychological abuse

"My ex-girlfriend was an emotional terrorist."

Overview

Emotional and psychological abuses tear a person up inside. They are disturbing, distracting, and debilitating. All other categories of abuse have an emotional/psychological component.

A woman may emotionally and psychologically abuse a man in a myriad of ways:

- isolation from friends, family, or other supportive people
- alienation of his children's affection
- minimizing his time with his children
- playing helpless
- abdicating responsibility for decision-making or her bad behavior
- making him feel responsible for the abuse
- neglect/withholding affection
- false accusations of abuse (of her or the children)
- harassment
- stalking
- character assassination
- manipulation
- distorting the truth
- unfounded jealousy
- gaslighting: trying to make him feel crazy
- unreasonable expectations
- false promises
- brainwashing
- corruption
- exploitation
- sabotaging his ability to have another relationship

Isolation

A woman is freer to control, punish, and/or demean her partner if she isolates him from friends, family, and other supportive people. She can try to undermine his relationship with his counselor or anyone else that might help him see her abuses or help him extract himself.

Possible methods of isolation include:

- creating physical isolation by instigating a move away from his family and friends,
- lying to him about his friends/family members to discredit them,
- accusing his friends/family of mistreating her,
- making him choose between his friends/family and her,
- complaining that any time he spends away from her is a hardship for her,
- insisting that all social time be spent with her friends and family,
- excessive jealousy,
- creating roadblocks to his ability to socialize, and
- badmouthing or threatening his therapist or anyone who might help him.

A woman insisted that her husband be home promptly after his work day ended to prove that he wasn't friendly with any women at work. She often berated him that he wasn't home fast enough and accused him of being unfaithful. Although he was absolutely faithful to her, he reduced contact with the outside world more and more in an attempt to appease her.

Another man's girlfriend intercepted emails sent to him by his friends and, without his knowledge at the time, replied to the emails as if she were him. By doing this, she very effectively controlled his contact with friends and undermined the relationships.

Early in yet another man's relationship with the woman who would become his wife (and eventually ex-wife), the woman accused his best friend of hitting on her. The accusation was presented to the man in private, not in front of the friend. The man immediately cut off all contact with his friend.

After they were married, this same woman told her husband that his mother and step-father had insulted her while they were visiting and he wasn't at home. When she presented him with the story, he became angry with his mother and confronted her. His mother was upset and tried to explain that the story wasn't true. In support of his wife, he stopped talking to his family.

Many years later, the man's eyes were opened to the reality of his wife's manipulations and he recognized that she had made the stories up to create rifts between him and anyone he loved or was close to.

Post-divorce, he became friendly with his ex's first husband and discovered that she had done the same thing to him.

Her first husband also described many instances of the shared ex isolating him from his friends and family. She would make up stories of mean things that his mother had supposedly said to her in his absence. His mother would deny doing what she was accused of, but he believed his then-wife. After his divorce, he went back and apologized to many friends and family members for having turned against them.

Alienation of his children's affection

Controversy has brewed over the idea of parental alienation since Richard Gardner described Parental Alienation Syndrome in the 1980s. The controversy largely focuses on whether or not there should be an official syndrome for children experiencing severe behavioral, psychological, and emotional impact from being manipulated into rejecting a loving, nurturing parent.

Whether or not there is an official syndrome, parents do sometimes choose to distort a child's reality so that the child is turned against the other parent in their efforts to control, punish, or demean the other parent. In so doing, they abuse both the child and the other parent.

What we are talking about here is different from normal estrangement that might occur between children and their parents because of expected stages of development or actual bad acts of the parents they are rejecting.

Intentional alienation of children's affection toward one parent can happen while a family is together, during separation, or after divorce. While the family is intact and living together, an abusive woman may maliciously work to undermine her partner's relationship with their child, misrepresenting the father's actions and attitudes, thereby distorting the child's perception of him. The most severe cases usually occur after separation or divorce.

Methods engaged by abusive women bent on creating a chasm between children and their father include:

- making the children think that her happiness is dependent on them choosing her over him;
- sabotaging his ability to spend time with them;

- lying about him or exaggerating his flaws;
- leading the children to believe he doesn't care about her or them;
- isolating the children from his extended family, including grandparents;
- interfering with their relationship with a step-mother; and
- forcing the children to lie about him.

Amy Baker, author of several books about parental alienation, describes a three-part message an alienating parent gives to their child:

1. I am the only parent who loves you, and you need me in order to feel good about yourself.
2. The other parent is dangerous and unavailable.
3. Pursuing a relationship with that parent jeopardizes your relationship with me.

In the most severe cases of alienation, the child fully adopts the alienating parent's hatred for the target parent.

When a man turned eighteen, his father showed him a shoebox of cashed child support checks. The existence of the checks went against everything the man had been told by his mother. After his parents divorced, his mother had filled his head with stories of how his father didn't care about him, including what he now knows were lies about non-payment of child support.

The father had tried and tried to secure time with the children, but his attempts were thwarted. The mother had so manipulated the situation that she demanded that the children lie about the father in court. Torn, but wanting to please her, the children had complied.

Minimizing his time with his children

In ideal situations, parents are both able to stay focused on the best interests of their children even if the relationship between the two of them isn't successful. After a breakup, a woman may wield a lot of control over the opportunities a father has to spend time with his children.

A selfish mother can turn children into her possessions and tools for hurting her former partner. Many men are tortured by custody battles and devastated by loss of contact with their children.

> A vindictive woman can deny a man contact with his stepchildren, and he has no legal recourse.

While some women get pregnant during dating to trap a husband, other women set out to have a relationship with a man just to get pregnant and then discard him, hoping he will go away and let her parent the child on her own. In this case, if the man wants to fulfill the role of father, the mother may put up roadblocks to minimize his time with the child.

To minimize a father's time with his children, a woman may:

- wage an unreasonable custody battle,
- falsely accuse him of being a bad father,
- withhold time with the children to punish him for "wrongdoing,"
- set up impossible conditions for visitation,
- not have the kids ready when it is his time to pick them up,
- not drop the kids off on time,
- make up stories about why his scheduled time with the children won't work out,

- move far away with the children, or even
- kidnap the children.

During a separation, a man's estranged wife was constantly threatening that if he didn't do this or that, he would not be able to pick up his son for his previously agreed-upon visitation.

Another man had a short fling with a woman. Even though the opportunity for her to conceive a child was very limited, she got pregnant. He was concerned for the welfare of his child and wanted to be a responsible, involved parent.

An intense energy-, money-, and time-consuming legal fight secured him his visitation and parental rights, but that was just the first phase of the struggle. Every opportunity the mother gets, or can create, she makes the visitations and his involvement as a parent difficult.

The mother sends him provocative, flirtatious text messages that cause him problems in his current relationship, even though he doesn't want to be with his son's mother and he tries to discourage her advances. In other texts and conversations she is demeaning and demanding.

The mother instigates endless changes to the visitation schedule. She doesn't have their son ready when it is time for pick-ups and isn't on time for drop-offs. Interactions with her about exchanges, and during exchanges, bounce back and forth between her being flirtatious and belligerent.

The father and his new partner are constantly on edge trying to keep up with the mother's nasty attitude and manipulations.

Playing helpless

Male training includes teaching them to protect and take care of women. While there is merit to this concept in healthy relationships and situations, a manipulative woman can capitalize on this cultural expectation by playing helpless in order to:

- entice and trap a man,
- coerce him to do things he doesn't want to do, and
- get him to carry an unreasonable degree of responsibility for the household and relationship.

A Damsel in Distress can have an intoxicating pull. A woman can sometimes get her way just by pouting or crying. Manipulative people can take tears to an art form. One woman bragged to her husband that she could manipulate men with ease: "All I have to do is act helpless, and they come running."

Many years ago, I was doing research for a series of articles I wrote about women's history and equality of the sexes. I read about, and then wrote about, the plight of women in the early 1900s, including that middle- and upper-class women were given few choices about their life and aspirations. They were expected to be married and taken care of by their husband.

In one of my articles, I wrote: "It was considered attractive to be frail and sickly; healthy women were even known to drink vinegar and arsenic in order to fulfill this image." I used to think, "Oh, those poor women. How awful to be forced to take arsenic to appear sickly so they could convince a man to marry them." Now I think, "How incredibly manipulative those women were to take arsenic so they could dupe men into thinking they were sickly and in need of their care."

> "You feel compelled
> to do what it takes
> to make her happy."

Men may be pulled into relationships with women who seem to need them and become trapped by the responsibility of taking care of them.

As one man explained: "You feel compelled to do what it takes to make her happy. You feel like a good person because you made her happy. She pretended she was unhappy to get me to save her. Then, she seemed to be relying on me, so how could I leave her?"

Another man describes his resistance to break free of his unhappy marriage with a dependent woman: "I feel like I would be a bad person if I leave this person."

Fake suicide attempts are the extreme skiing of the helplessness sport.* Many a man has married the woman who "attempted suicide" because she couldn't live without him after he broke up with her. Many of those same men end up divorcing that woman after five to thirty years of married manipulation.

*I'm *not* advocating ignoring suicidal gestures or attempts; nor am I making light of genuine suicidal gestures, attempts, or completions. I am speaking about the abusive use of this serious subject with the intent to manipulate and entrap caring people.

For more about suicide, see Chapter 30, *Resources*.

Abdicating responsibility

Merriam-Webster.com defines *abdicating* as failure to do what is required by a duty or responsibility.

Abdicating responsibility in relationships can take on several forms:

- unwillingness to contribute to, or make, decisions
- not taking on a fair share of duties
- not taking responsibility for one's own actions

A woman who is unwilling to take responsibility for decision-making burdens her partner by forcing him to carry a disproportionate share of responsibility. Her abdication can be presented as innocuously as: "I don't care." "Do whatever you want to do." "We'll go wherever you want to go." In abusive situations, these statements are often a set-up for criticizing him for decisions he was compelled to make that don't turn out to her liking.

Not taking on a fair share of duties that need to be performed to keep a family going dumps those responsibilities on the other partner.

When someone doesn't take responsibility for her own actions, there isn't introspection or trying to figure out how things could improve; instead, there are excuses or blaming of others. The "other" that is blamed for whatever she did is often her partner. He can be blamed for anything she has done, including her abusive actions: "I wouldn't have done _____, if you hadn't done _____."

> She may blame him for her *need* to be abusive: "I wouldn't have done _____, if you hadn't done _____."

A man was kept spinning by doing everything. He ran a business, took care of the household duties, made sure their daughter got to ballet . . . He was a very capable guy and for many years bolstered himself by repeatedly telling himself, "I can do it. I need to do it."

His wife could barely get to work on time. There always seemed to be someone at work that was to blame for her being in trouble there.

She was diagnosed with an illness, but didn't take her prescribed medication regularly and wouldn't stop consuming the alcohol that was clearly able to mess with that medication.

While he was working as hard as humanly possible to juggle all the responsibilities, she was ultra-critical of him. So many things didn't meet with her approval, and she vociferously let him know.

A side effect of all of this was that he was kept so busy that he didn't have any capacity leftover to see what was really going on. He was consumed by dealing with one disaster, after another, after another.

He couldn't see that she was contributing to her own ill health. He couldn't see that she was distorting the truth in her everyone-else-but-me-is-responsible work stories.

He kept thinking that if he was just good enough, things would go well and she would be happy.

Neglect and Withholding affection

Some people won't give their partners the time of day. It can leave the neglected partner feeling fatally flawed, thirsty for attention, and eager to do whatever it takes so that they are worthy of that attention.

A partner may withhold affection as a method to extract wanted behavior from her partner. The partner receives the reward of attention or demonstrations of affection when he does whatever she wants him to do.

Sometimes the lack of attention is the result of depression or a selfish lack of caring about the partner. Sometimes there is an active withholding of affection or attention to punish, demean, or control, such as with the cold shoulder"or the silent treatment.

Neglect and the withholding of affection are particularly difficult forms of abuse to spot. They are the absence of something rather than the presence of something.

"Neglect is death by a thousand cuts."

A man struggled for years with his feelings of being neglected by his wife. She would leave the house without telling him where she was going or even an indication that she was leaving. She didn't want to have anything to do with sex (although that wasn't the case when they were dating). She would make lunch plans with him but then cancel at the last minute if something "better" came up.

This man felt like he was nothing more than a meal ticket for his wife. He described the neglect as "death by a thousand cuts."

False accusations of abuse

An abusive woman may pull an end-around play by falsely accusing the man she abuses of abusing her. It's a mesmerizing circular move.

False accusations of abuse of her or the children can be conjured up to punish, demean, or exert control over a partner or former partner. They can be used to extort favorable settlements; to discredit him with family, friends, employers, customers, and divorce adjudicators; or to get him in legal hot water.

> It pains a nice guy to be lumped in with members of his gender that do things he finds abhorrent.

Threats of leveling false accusations are effective mechanisms of control. The last thing a nice guy wants is to be lumped in with members of his gender that do things he finds abhorrent. The thought of having to battle an abuse charge in the current cultural climate can strike fear in any man.

A manipulative woman who had decided she wanted to end her marriage threatened her husband, declaring that if he didn't give in to her financial demands, "I'll make life miserable for you! I'll run you out of town!"

She made up stories presenting herself as her husband's victim. She told her parents that her husband had yelled at her and been threatening. Her father was aghast and very angry with his "mean" son-in-law.

The false accusation of abuse motivated the father to try to protect his daughter and helped cement the father-daughter relationship. The father joined in the spreading of the abuse stories in the community, trying to undermine the husband's customer base.

The wife sprinkled her divorce court declarations with twisted, distorted stories that depicted her estranged husband as an abuser. While this divorce was in a no-fault state (supposedly the causes of deterioration of the marriage don't matter), painting the man as an abuser was intended to color the judge's opinion of the husband and result in judgments favorable to the "poor" wife.

A Texas woman took false accusations against her husband in a different direction. She abused other people, very important visible people, and accused her husband, Nathan Richardson, of being the abuser.

In 2013, she mailed ricin-laced letters to the President of the United States and the Mayor of New York City. (Ricin is an extremely lethal poison.) After the letters were sent, she approached law enforcement with the accusation that her husband had mailed the letters.

It didn't take officers long to figure out that she, not her husband, was behind the poison letters, which were mailed shortly after Nathan filed for divorce. Evidence against her included that he was at work when pertinent Internet searches were performed on the home computer, and when envelopes were postmarked. She had little choice but to admit her involvement. But, of course, in her revised story she said he made her do it.

Six months after the incident, she pled guilty to the charges. She made a plea agreement capping her sentence at eighteen years while acknowledging that she "obtained an email address, a PayPal shopping account and a post office box in her husband's name without his knowledge."[1]

Harassment and Stalking

Harassment is obsessive contact or monitoring of a person. It is often based in a need to control, demean, or punish the object of the harassment. It can be in the form of incessant phone calls, text messages, or emails that don't stop even when you have clearly stated that you want them to stop.

A man's wife knew the timing of each of his work breaks. She'd call him during each break. If he didn't answer the call, she'd be all over him with accusations and putdowns. She knew when his shift was over. He had to call her immediately or she would accuse him of being with a girlfriend. (He didn't have a girlfriend.)

When he went to visit his family, they'd see him sitting in his car for long periods of time talking to his wife on the phone. She'd be screaming at him over the phone: "You love them more than you love me!"

Stalking is repeated following or monitoring of another person in a harassing manner. Stalking can occur during a relationship or after it ends. A stalking partner or ex-partner can perform the surveillance themselves, engage family or friends to perform the job, or hire someone to do it.

The term "stalking" implies behavior beyond a reasonable level of checking out rational suspicions that a partner is being deceptive. It implies obsessive, controlling, and/or punishing behavior.

Stalking can be physical or it can occur online in the form of cyber-stalking. Social media offers up a whole realm of harassment possibilities, from the posting of demeaning comments to revenge porn (posting naked pictures of an ex after a breakup).

Character assassination

An abusive woman can become very angry and vengeful when a relationship ends. Even if she treated her partner with disdain when they were together, she may have the attitude: "How dare you not want to be with me!" Spreading his secrets, or lies and distortions about his character, can become her main goal in life.

The advent of social media and email has made it relatively easy for a vengeful woman to spread a wide negative net quickly. Many men have suffered through disparaging Internet campaigns waged by exes bent on ruining their reputation, undermining their relationships with family, friends, or co-workers, and jeopardizing their jobs.

Jodi Arias is the most glaring example of character assassination of a romantic partner. Jodi brutally murdered her former boyfriend, Travis Alexander, in 2008. Stabbing Travis over 25 times, slitting his throat, and shooting him in the head weren't enough for Jodi. After killing Travis physically, she attempted to kill his character.

Jodi set out to *destroy* Travis and everyone's image of him. In day upon day of trial testimony, Jodi attempted to convince the jury (and the television audience) that Travis was manipulative, cruel, perverted, and deserving of death.

Her version of Travis didn't fit with how most people saw him, but some listeners were taken in by her stories. She was able to secure a domestic violence professional to back up her claim for innocent victim status. The jury didn't let her sway them from a murder conviction, but at the writing of this book it remains to be seen whether her stories will help dissuade them from sentencing her to death.

Manipulation

Manipulative people do a sales job on you. They are selling you on whatever they want you to do or think. They can use illusion, coercion, enticement, intimidation, and/or sex, because as everyone knows, "sex sells."

They can use a carrot-and-stick approach of rewarding desired behavior and punishing undesired behavior. The rewards and punishments may be obvious or subtle and coy.

A woman may reward her partner for desired behavior directly with sex, money, smiles . . . Or she may reward him indirectly by temporarily curtailing her own undesirable behavior (the sad-puppy-dog look, yelling, threatening . . .).

> "Manipulation is always one-sided, asymmetrical, or unbalanced in its motivation. Once the line between appropriate influence and manipulation has been crossed, relationships become disturbed and troubled."
> —Harriet Braiker,
> *Who's Pulling Your Strings*

The punishment may be that there is a price to pay if she doesn't get her way. That price may be no sex, the silent treatment, pouting, hitting, or some other unpleasant or dangerous consequence.

A manipulative partner has time and accessibility on her side. She can experiment to find the techniques that get her boyfriend, husband, or ex to do what she wants him to do. If he becomes immune to one of her methods, she can devise and practice another way to get what she wants.

There is a manipulative component to many abusive behaviors/attitudes.

Distorting the truth

Distortions of truth may be used by an abusive woman to cover her tracks, create an illusion, distract from reality, make herself look good or her partner look bad, garner sympathy or advantage . . . The goal may be to alter the partner's perception of the situation, or to give false impressions to other people about herself or her partner.

Distortions may also be used as a source of fun. Some people enjoy the game of pulling the wool over other people's eyes. It makes them feel powerful. It's exhilarating.

> "Everyone has a right to their own opinion, but not to their own facts."
> —Ricky Gervais

Distorting the truth can take on many forms:

- pretending she is someone she is not
- creating a cover story
- "Me thinks thou doth protest too much"
- burying the lead
- telling half-truths
- diverting
- minimizing
- exaggerating
- denying the truth
- withholding information
- selective memory
- straight-up lying

Pretending she is someone she is not

She weaves stories that present her as someone very different than reality in order to hook a man or hide her true self during the relationship.

Creating a cover story

She presents a story about her whereabouts/actions or someone else's actions with the goal of preempting doubts or concerns her partner may have about her.

"Me thinks thou doth protest too much"

She goes out of her way to talk about how abhorrent a particular behavior is while she is secretly doing that same thing.

Burying the lead

She discloses that she has done something not-good but it's said quietly, when he's distracted, or buried in amongst other information; then she can safely assume he won't hear it, but she can say she said it.

Telling half-truths

She says things that are partially true with a flair and twist, leading the hearer to draw conclusions that aren't true.

Diverting

She changes the subject when her partner is honing in on something she doesn't want him to know.

Minimizing

She minimizes her wrongdoing to make it seem less important or "bad" than it really is, and/or she minimizes her partners accomplishments and attributes to make him seem less "good."

Exaggerating

She exaggerates her accomplishments, contributions, abilities . . ., and/or she exaggerates his shortcomings.

Denying the truth

She claims that that which is true—is false.

Withholding information

She lies by omission rather than commission.

Selective memory

She claims that conversations or events that happened didn't happen.

Straight-up lying

As one man described his wife: "If her lips are moving, she's lying."

After a man separated from his wife, he "kept unveiling deeper levels of deception."

His wife lied at the beginning of their relationship as she was wooing him. He was taken in by her stories at the time, but would discover much later that they were exaggerations and distortions. During their marriage, she would often go on and on about how bad people are who cheat on their spouses, while, in reality, *she* was cheating on *him*. She moved money into a bank account that he didn't know about until forensic accounting discovered it during the divorce. These deceits were just the tip of the iceberg.

Unfounded jealousy

It would not be surprising if a woman felt some jealousy if she found out that her partner was having an affair or even if she had rational reason to suspect he was having an affair. That would be part of a normal reaction.

Unfounded jealousy is not that rational. It's obsessive. It's much more about the jealous person than it is about the target of the jealousy. It's used as an excuse to control, demean, or punish.

A man's wife was incessantly jealous even though he did nothing to warrant the jealousy. The list of what set off her jealousy was long and ever-growing.

She insisted that he cut off all contact with any woman he had been friends with prior to their relationship. She monitored for any such contact.

She insisted that he have no personal or friendly interactions with the women he worked with. If he arrived home from work later than she expected, she came at him with the vehemence of an inquisitor.

She banned him from going to the gym because there would be women in skimpy, tight clothes there.

One day, as the couple was driving down the road, he happened to look out the window as a woman walked by. His inadvertent glance in the direction of another woman became fodder for criticism that went on for months.

This wife used jealousy to control her husband's time and space. She used it as an excuse to belittle him. She used it to berate and punish him.

Gaslighting

Gaslight is a play by Patrick Hamilton set in the era when gas lamps lit homes and streets. It was adapted into a movie in 1944. The term *gaslighting*, which refers to trying to make your partner feel crazy, was created based on the story's depiction of a man trying to do just that.

The male lead character sets up his wife, Paula, to slowly undermine her belief in her perceptions of things. He moves items from where she put them and then criticizes her for "losing" them. He creates the illusion that he is

> "Suddenly, I'm beginning not to trust my memory at all."
> –Paula, in *Gaslight*

leaving the house every night, but doubles back to enter the attic so that he can search through her dead aunt's things looking for valuable jewels. He accuses his wife of being delusional to explain the footsteps she hears in the attic and the dimming of the house gaslights caused by him turning on the attic lamp.

Gaslighting occurs when someone intentionally twists your perception of reality for their own gain. That gain may be to win a fight, cover-up their actions, make you think something is true when it is not or think something is false when it is true, or undermine your trust in yourself.

A gaslighting woman may try to convince you that:

- what you saw, you didn't see,
- what you said, you didn't say,
- what you heard, you didn't hear,
- what you didn't see, you saw,
- what you didn't say, you said, or
- what you didn't hear, was there for the hearing.

Unreasonable expectations

There are two sides to the unreasonable expectations coin:

- she has unreasonable expectations
- she labels his reasonable expectations as unreasonable

Both sides of the unreasonable expectations coin are grounded in the principle that she is more important than he is. What she wants is more important than what he wants. Her wants get exaggerated into needs. His wants and needs get minimized and negated.

There are repercussions if an abusive woman's expectations aren't met. She may yell, pout, cry, hit, go silent, withhold sex . . .

Unreasonable expectations often contain absolutes: *always*, *never*, *all*, or *none*. Unreasonable expectations may be rooted in maliciousness, selfishness, or a lack of awareness.

her reasonable expectation	her unreasonable expectation
she expects some of his attention	she expects all of his attention
she expects to decide together what each of their financial contributions should be during different phases of their relationship	she expects to be financially carried by him regardless of family circumstances or their capacities to earn
she expects him to spend a lot of his free time with her	she expects him to spend all of his free time with her
she expects him to have some input into how she spends her time	she expects to do whatever she wants whenever she wants

False promises

False promises is a torture technique used on prisoners of war and on romantic partners. With a false promise, the target is set up to believe that something good is going to happen, he develops hopeful anticipation of it happening, and then the rug is pulled out from underneath him. The dashed hopes take the target down to a much lower emotional low than before the promise was made.

> A false promise
> may be stated or implied.

This torture technique was described to me as one used by the Vietnamese on American POWs. The scenario went something like this:

- A prisoner is told he is going home in a month.
- The promise is reinforced regularly.
- At three weeks, there is paperwork to be done because he is "going home."
- At two weeks, there is something else that needs to be completed because he is "going home."
- They keep up the ruse to the point of even putting him on a plane ostensibly bound for home.
- On the plane the prisoner is informed that he isn't going home. He's told, "they don't want you" because he did this or that wrong.
- The emotional devastation the prisoner experiences takes him to a much deeper emotional low than where he was before the promise was made.

With cyclical partner abuse, each spin around the abuse cycle includes a stated or implied promise of change. The promise is followed by an increase in tension, repeat of abusive behavior, and the corresponding psychological low of dashed hopes in the target of the abuse.

Brainwashing

Like false promises, brainwashing is an example of how abuse in relationships parallels torture. Abusive people are often able to throw the targets of their abuse into a trance that makes it difficult for them to think clearly. Targets of abuse can begin to take on the opinions of the abusive person and lose themselves.

A man who is peppered with his partner's opinion, given little or no time to recover, and kept busy responding to demands may not have much mental energy left over. He may be inundated with her version of events to the point where it is difficult to hold on to his perspective. The anxiety that can be produced by being the target of abuse also makes it difficult to think clearly.

Brainwashing is defined in the *Psychology Dictionary* as that which "manipulates and modifies a person's emotions, attitudes, and beliefs." Brainwashing reduces a person's ability to mentally defend himself and makes it easier for another person to control him.

In 1956, Albert Biderman studied how POW camp personnel got US prisoners of the Korean War to give them tactical information, collaborate with propaganda, and agree with false confessions. Biderman stated that inflicting physical pain was not necessary to "induce compliance," but psychological manipulations were extremely effective for that purpose. His report included what has come to be known as *Biderman's Chart of Coercion*.

Biderman's chart has been used by many to describe the elements that contribute to brainwashing in various situations including partner abuse. The tactics included in his chart are linkable to other ways women abuse men.

In his Chart of Coercion,[2] Biderman summarized the mechanisms for brainwashing:

1. Isolation
2. Monopolization of perception (fixes attention on immediate predicament; eliminates "undesirable" stimuli)
3. Induced debilitation; exhaustion
4. Threats
5. Occasional indulgences (provides motivation for compliance; hinders adjustment to deprivation)
6. Demonstrating superiority
7. Degradation
8. Enforcing trivial demands

Not all eight elements need to be present in order for brainwashing to occur. Each element can be seen to have some power to distort reality, interfere with perception, reduce a person's self-confidence, and garner compliance.

In a POW camp, the prisoner and jailer are enemies. Service men and women are commonly trained to deal with brainwashing tactics in case they are captured by enemy forces.

In a romantic relationship, the partners are supposed to be on the same side. It is reasonable to expect love, understanding, and compassion from your partner, and to want to offer that to her also. The relationship, unfortunately, creates a vulnerability to the coercive brainwashing of a malicious or self-centered partner. It is unexpected. It can sneak up on you.

Corruption

To *corrupt* (from TheFreeDictionary.com):

- "to destroy or subvert the honesty or integrity of"
- "to ruin morally; pervert; taint; contaminate"

The brainwashing aspect of partner abuse sets up the potential of a man blindly following his partner and being unduly influenced by her opinion. Her hold on him may make it relatively easy for her to persuade him to go against his values or develop destructive interests he would not venture towards on his own.

A woman may use sex as an efficient mechanism to get a man to do things he would not normally do. The perversion of his morals may be directly related to sex, in that it involves sexual activity he would normally consider immoral, or the woman may use sex to subvert his rational thinking and render him more malleable to follow her lead.

The Damsel in Distress act is another means to control a man and cloud his thinking ability. A man may be willing to do things to save the damsel from her plight that he would not do under other circumstances.

There are many ways a woman might corrupt her partner:

- get him involved in drugs, sex, gambling . . .
- undermine an alcoholic partner's sobriety by encouraging him to drink or partying in front of him
- corrupt his view and treatment of friends and family
- convince him to lie for her
- manipulate a boyfriend into helping her kill or destroy her husband

Exploitation

Exploitation is defined as:

- "treating someone unfairly in order to benefit from their work" (OxfordDictionaries.com),
- "selfish utilization" (Dictionary.com), and
- "to make use of meanly or unfairly for one's own advantage" (Merriam-Webster.com).

Manipulative, self-centered women may exploit men in a myriad of ways, including exploiting their:

- position,
- money,
- time,
- energy,
- good nature,
- male training to be a provider and protector, or
- inexperience.

A woman spotted a man who had proven himself to be committed, smart, and inexperienced at relationships. She pursued him relentlessly. Shortly after they began dating, she started moving her things into his house a bit at a time. Soon, she had her young daughter spending the night. Almost before he realized what was going on, both the mother and daughter had moved in.

She pushed for marriage. He gave in. She pushed for them to have a child. He protested, but she got her way. She quit her job. He worked long hours at his career, did the housework, and ran the kids to their activities. She played computer games, siphoned money off into her secret bank accounts, and complained about how tired she was.

If I can't have you, then no one will!

A malicious soon-to-be-ex or ex may try to sabotage her man's ability to have a new partner. She may:

- work to make the man financially unattractive by ruining his credit, leaving him with debt, racking up legal fees, walking away with most of the assets, or extracting extended oversized support payments;
- be flirtatious to stir up jealousy in his new partner;
- verbally attack his new partner directly or try to discredit her with family, friends, or community;
- undermine the new partner's relationship with the children;
- create drama and chaos to distract him and wear out any new partners; or
- disparage the man in the community, trying to tarnish his reputation and decrease the likelihood another woman will find him attractive.

The most violent manifestation of the concept of "If I can't have you, then no one will!" is murder. In 2002, Clara Harris ran over her husband, David, with her Mercedes when she discovered he was having an affair. Clara claimed that "it was an accident," but the police report, and video taken by the private investigator Clara had hired to follow her husband, showed that she ran over her husband multiple times. David died from his wounds while his 16-year-old daughter from a previous marriage looked on.

While the story of David Harris is violent and tragic, many women try to kill the targets of their abuse in ways that are not so direct—they attempt to kill their psyche, their ability to thrive, their spirit, or their future.

Part Three

Why women abuse men

Part Three

Why they do it

Reasons for behavior explain behavior.
They don't excuse the behavior.

The overarching conscious or subconscious goals of partner abuse are to demean, control, or punish; but why does a particular woman treat her partner that way?

We are each made up of our biology (genetics and health), everything that's ever happened to us, and everything we've ever been exposed to. That combination creates our thoughts—both conscious and subconscious—and feelings in the moment. Thoughts and feelings lead to behavior.

People always have reasons for thinking what they think and doing what they do. They may not be good or healthy reasons. They may not be rational or logical reasons. They may not be conscious reasons.

There is a long list of possible answers to the question of why a particular woman exhibits potentially abusive behaviors toward her male partner. She may be anything from well-intentioned but unaware that what she is doing is as destructive as it is—to being a full-blown malicious sociopath.

Knowing why someone does something can help you understand that person better and help them understand themselves better. But understanding why isn't the end of it. Reasons for behavior don't excuse behavior. There has to be a willingness to use the information found in the "why" to figure out how to change.

Adults are responsible for recognizing when their behaviors and attitudes are harmful to themselves or others and then doing the work to figure out how to stop. At some point, it no longer matters why she does what she does; it only matters whether she chooses to change and whether her partner is up for giving her another chance.

A combination of factors may work together to create an individual's abusive behaviors and attitudes, or there may be one predominant reason.

A woman may have learned abusive behaviors from:

- being pampered as a child,
- being abused as a child,
- being bullied,
- bullying others,
- previous abuse by another man,
- witnessing her father abuse her mother,
- witnessing her mother abuse her father, or
- cultural sanction, even encouragement, of the abuse of men by women.

She may lack skill in:

- dealing with emotions,
- taking care of herself,
- managing her anger,
- budgeting money,
- being assertive, or
- communication.

> Reasons for behavior don't excuse behavior.

She may be any of the following:

- frustrated
- exhausted
- stressed
- feeling threatened (emotionally, mentally, physically, financially . . .)
- confusing aggression with assertiveness
- driven by dichotomous thinking
- unaware of the effect of her actions

- insecure
- overreactive
- a perfectionist
- an adrenaline junkie
- hormonally challenged
- projecting her own ways of thinking, doing, or being onto him
- lazy
- addicted to shopping, gambling, sex . . .
- abusing alcohol or drugs
- self-centered
- a man-hater
- drawn to the game of abuse
- histrionic
- narcissistic
- sociopathic
- just plain mean

She may have:

- low self-esteem,
- poor impulse control,
- physical illness,
- a brain injury,
- dementia,
- depression,
- anxiety,
- a bipolar disorder,
- posttraumatic stress, or
- borderline personality.

She may want to:

- be heard,
- get his attention,
- better her position,
- get her way,
- punish him for his "wrongs,"
- punish this man for the "wrongs" of men in general or another man in particular,
- compensate for past experiences of not having control over her life,
- push the target of her abuse into doing something "bad,"
- avoid responsibility,
- feel superior,
- trap her man,
- distract from something she has done,
- attain victim status, or
- feel powerful.

She may be motivated by:

- fear,
- self-defense,
- need to protect others,
- love (potentially distorted love),
- hatred,
- selfishness,
- jealousy,
- personal gain (status, legal, financial . . .),
- retaliation,
- revenge (for real or imagined wrongs), or
- obsession.

Chapter 12

Taught and thought

"It's surprising how many persons go through life
without ever recognizing that
their feelings toward other people
are largely determined by their feelings toward themselves,
and if you're not comfortable within yourself,
you can't be comfortable with others."

—Sidney J. Harris

Set up to be abusive

Early life, or any portion of her life that predates the current situation, may set a woman up to be abusive. The set up may be:

- collateral (she observed abuse),
- reactionary (she was abused herself), or
- direct (she was encouraged to abuse).

Collateral

Abusive behaviors may be modeled by parents in the way that they treat each other or the children. A person raised in that environment may be trained to handle relationships in the same way.

> Sometimes the abused becomes the abuser.

Reactionary

A woman who is abusive may have been the target of abuse herself earlier in her life. She may have been abused by her parents, siblings, caregiver, a stranger, or a previous partner. She may have been bullied by peers.

Previous abuse by a male may turn a woman into a man-hater. In that case, her anger toward the man that hurt her is generalized to all men. She may even seek out men to ensnarl and abuse.

Direct

Abusive behavior may be adopted as the way to be by someone who participates in a group culture that includes the bullying of others, or who is trained to expect to have her own way.

Sometimes a woman is abusive towards her partner because she has been pampered by the family that raised her or people around her. She may be accustomed to being deferred to, coddled, overindulged, and taken care of.

> Sometimes abusive behaviors are cultivated by being raised as a princess.

She may be used to being treated like a princess and have the unreasonable expectation of reigning over her partner.

A couple of points of clarification:

- Not all people who were abused become abusive.
- Not all people who are abusive were abused (or pampered).

It is by no means a given that an abused person will become abusive.

There is a whole spectrum of possible outcomes from having been previously abused. An abused person may seek out better ways of treating herself and others. Another possibility is that she becomes passive because of being trained into that role, or in an attempt to distance herself from being the type of person that hurt her.

How a person was treated earlier in life is just one potential contributing factor to that individual's attitudes and behaviors. Other potential contributing factors include genetics, health, education, finances, recent life experiences and exposures, culture, and everything else on the long list in Chapter 11, *Why they do it.*

Cultural sanction of abuse

Media representations of the relationships of men and women reflect and reinforce cultural norms and beliefs. For many years, there has been a trend for TV commercials to depict men as wrong, bad, stupid, lazy, clumsy idiots in need of a woman to set them straight. Women in these commercials are presented as smart and active authorities. Women's controlling, demeaning, and punishing treatment of men is portrayed as expected and justified.

If these characterizations of the relative qualities of men and women and how they interact with each other were rare, they could be discounted as not telling us much. It's the frequency of the depictions that reveals their significance. The lack of reverse scenarios is also revealing. We are not likely to see a company using a man demeaning or slapping a woman as a way to promote their product.

While I was working on this section, I saw yet another of these commercials that glorifies females dominating over males. The commercial opens with a middle-aged woman gardening in a nice neighborhood. Her younger self appears and reminds her how she used to reward herself with a Little Debbie treat when she finished a task.

The woman excitedly drops her flowers and runs to the kitchen, where she finds her husband just about to take a bite of a cupcake. She grabs the treat out of her husband's hand and declares, "You can have one when you finish cleaning out the garage."

They're not done yet. In the next shot, as the woman sits relaxing, enjoying the cupcake she confiscated from her husband, her younger self says to her, "You should get him to do the attic too." The two age-versions of the woman fist bump each other to confirm what a great idea it is for her to control and demean her husband, doling out the rules and rewards.

These commercials that use the woman-lording-over-a-man format contribute to, and expose, the invisibleness of the abuse of men by women. We are acclimatized to it. We expect it. We find it amusing.

At a gathering of local writers, the guest of honor was a petite, distinguished-looking silver-haired woman who has published many books and had several of her works turned into movies. I was introduced to her at the same time as a couple of other people. We all stood in close proximity, explaining our areas of interest for our writing.

I told them I was writing books on communication skills, relationship skills, and the abuse of men by women. The accomplished guest author blurted out: "When it's a movie, I want to play the woman. There are a couple of men I'd like to abuse." This woman, who clearly knows how to use words and choose them wisely, had no shame or second thought in asserting her support of abuse of men in front of a number of strangers in a professional setting.

Unfortunately, that author's attitude is very widespread. Extra-unfortunately, the pro-abuse stance regarding women abusing men has also infiltrated the professions that are in the best position to counsel men who are abused and women who are abusive.

A social worker asked me about my counseling work. I said that I work with adult men and women as individuals and couples, and that my areas of expertise include the abuse of men by women. Her response: "The pendulum just has to swing in that way because men have abused women."

Low self-esteem

Low self-esteem has a whole continuum of possible repercussions, from squelching all motivation to creating an insatiable drive for achievement and dominance. On one end of the continuum, people with low self-esteem may appear downtrodden, and on the other end, they may put on airs of superiority.

Healthy self-esteem is: "I am lovable" and "I am capable of handling myself in my environment."

Self-esteem is *not* about the face that someone shows to the world. Even people who appear to have it all may have low self-esteem. Self-esteem is about what someone feels inside, at their core.

People with low self-esteem may rebuff compliments and resist absorbing signs that they are worthy of feeling OK about themselves. Like a wood-chipper takes in wood, churns it up and spits it out, and then is empty again, a person with low self-esteem may take their partner's compliments and offerings of love, churn them up, and spit them out, and then be empty again, needing more.

If a woman doesn't feel good about herself, she has many options for dealing with that uncomfortable feeling. She can choose to:

- grin and bear it,
- work on figuring out why and build her self-esteem up to a healthy level,
- criticize other people so she can feel superior,
- dominate other people in attempts to inflate her ego,
- inflate her sense of self by boasting, or
- wallow in self-pity and helplessness.

Dichotomous thinking

Dichotomous thinking is black-or-white, all-or-nothing thinking. "Di" means two. With dichotomous thinking, there are only two options.

It is not a very real way of viewing the world. Most things in reality have more than two options. Most situations have a whole continuum of possibilities between the two polar opposites.

Even if we take black and white as the epitome of dichotomous thinking, most of what we label black and white isn't 100% black or 100% white. Most of what we call black and white would actually fall somewhere within the continuum that represents the mixture of each. And there is the whole grey scale in between that is the combination of different degrees of black and white.

Dichotomous thinking is a mind trap. It only allows for a right and a wrong. It pushes people to be driven towards the absolute opposite of what they don't want to be. With dichotomous thinking: either she's right and he's wrong, or he's right and she's wrong. There are only two options. If she doesn't like being "wrong," she has to always be "right."

It creates an all-or-nothing view that distorts situations into absolutes. Absolutes are often said, and felt, while ignoring exceptions to the absolutes. Examples of absolutes:

- "You *never* pick up your underwear."
- "You're *always* late."
- "You don't care about me." (In this one, *not at all* is implied.)

Confusing aggression with assertiveness

Dichotomous thinking may contribute to aggressive behaviors and attitudes being mislabeled as assertiveness.

Assertiveness is not aggression. Assertiveness is being able to say what you have to say with tact. It's standing up for yourself and others—with a combination of honesty and respect. And it's being able to decide when it's appropriate to voice your thoughts and feelings.

On the assertiveness continuum, *assertive* is the middle area, *passive* is on one end, and *aggressive* is on the other end:

passive	**ASSERTIVE**	aggressive

Dichotomous thinking can lead someone to conclude that there are only two options: be walked all over or be aggressive. She may become aggressive to protect herself from being passive, or vice versa (become passive to protect herself from being aggressive).

Sometimes people bounce back and forth between passive and aggressive. In that case, it may look like:

> take it,
> take it,
> take it,
> explode!

In reality, both ends of this continuum are unhealthy; healthy lies in the middle of the continuum between *passive* and *aggressive*. Assertiveness is the healthy, balanced approach to communication. It is an attitude and skill that needs to be learned.

Perfectionism

Perfectionism is another outcropping of dichotomous thinking. Not all people who have a dichotomous view of the world are perfectionists, but most perfectionists are dichotomous thinkers.

Perfectionism is a tough taskmaster. No one can be perfect. Things can't go perfectly. Perfectionists are chronically frustrated and disappointed with themselves and with the people close to them.

Excellence is a worthy goal. Perfection is not. Excellence is achieving to the best of your ability under the circumstances.

Here's a look at the excellence continuum:

abject failure	**EXCELLENCE**	perfection

Dichotomous thinkers might think that being anything less than perfect means they are an abject failure. In reality, both ends of this continuum are unhealthy. Abject failure is clearly not a good place to be, and perfection is unattainable; healthy lies somewhere in the middle.

There are other labels that could be used for the ends of the continuum.

The *perfection* end of the continuum could have many labels:

- unflawed
- spotless
- pure
- untarnished

- undefiled
- faultless
- blameless
- undamaged
- unfaultable
- irreproachable

The *abject failure* end of the continuum could also have many labels:

- lazy
- useless
- worthless
- defective
- pathetic
- slovenly
- damaged
- loser

If a person feels "not good enough," dichotomous thinking can drive her to perfection in attempts to quiet that fatally flawed feeling. Everything short of perfection can pick at that wound and be intolerably painful.

> "When your personal rule (spoken or unspoken) is that everything you need to do needs to be perfect, failure is inevitable."
> —Curt Rosengren,
> *U.S. News & World Report*

A woman who is a perfectionist may see people who are close to her, such as her children or partner, as representative of her. She may demand perfection from them because anything short of perfection in them stimulates her to feel like she is an abject failure.

Miscellaneous unhealthy reasons

Some people who are abusive are **just plain mean**. They are driven to put others down, exert control, and/or punish. Their way of being may be rooted in habit or invisible payoff. They get some satisfaction from being mean.

Some are drawn to **the game** of abuse like a cat playing with a cornered mouse. It may be the feeling of having power over someone, or the intrigue, or the challenge. It may be entertainment for them.

A particular woman may be driven by **selfishness**. She may be singularly focused on getting her own way and have learned abusive tactics achieve that goal. Her methods work for her but take a toll on a partner who might have wants and needs in conflict with hers.

Revenge or retaliation may create unchecked motivation for a woman to abuse. It may be in response to something real or imagined that her partner did recently or long ago. It may not have anything to do with her current partner, but rather be in response to events from her past involving different people and circumstances. In that case, the current partner is made to suffer for the "wrongs" of others.

A person who has a **position of authority at work** may be bossy, controlling, and demanding with her partner because she has transferred her work position and personality to her home life. This can happen with managers, police officers, educators, and others.

Emotional reasons

"Heav'n has no rage, like love to hatred turn'd,
nor hell a fury, like a woman scorn'd."

—William Congreve,
from the play *The Mourning Bride* (1697)

Overreactions

Emotional overreactions are more emotion than the amount warranted by whatever just happened. Overreactions occur when a person taps into stored emotion and feels not only the emotion that goes with what just happened, but also a whole lot of stored emotion. It can stimulate a small burst of overreaction or a torrent.

Sometimes emotional overreactions are outward and dramatic; sometimes they are barely visible to the outside world but pack an inner punch.

A person having an overreaction can mistakenly think that all the emotion they are feeling is about what just happened. They can then conclude what just happened "must be terrible!" because it caused all this pain. And they may think that whoever else was involved "must be terrible!" because they caused all this pain.

> A person experiencing an overreaction can mistakenly think that all the emotion they are feeling is about whatever just happened.

In reality, the amount of emotion isn't only about what just happened; it's also about the emotional accumulation from old events. Those other events may be a few minutes old. They may be years old. They may be connected to the same people or things, or they may have nothing to do with them.

One of the challenges with overreactions is to determine how much of the emotional response is directly connected to what just happened. The answer to that question can be anywhere from "nearly nothing" to "most of it."

There are two sources of emotional overreactions:

- Direct Hit
- Add-On

Direct Hit

In the case of a Direct Hit, the overreaction occurs because the current emotion is connecting to that same emotion from another time. The past events may be recent or long ago. They may be connected to the same players or different people entirely.

For example, if she seems to be overreacting to you talking to your female friend, even though this particular situation is genuinely innocent, she may be tapping into times in the past that you betrayed her or times in the past when she felt betrayed by someone else.

Add-On

The Add-On effect happens when several emotions are triggered in close time proximity to each other or are connected to that same person or situation. They accumulate. It's the last one in that creates the overflow and can be mistaken for the source of all the emotional pain.

Feeling powerless at work, adds to fear of being late, adds to frustration that the cap got left off the toothpaste. She's screaming at you about the toothpaste or is drenched in tears and you're wondering why all the fuss about toothpaste. It's not really about the toothpaste. It's everything coming together in that moment.

Anger

Anger is a secondary emotion. Some sort of emotional pain or discomfort (fear, rejection, shame . . .) isn't getting dealt with directly and is being turned into anger.

Anger begs the question, "What emotional discomfort isn't getting dealt with directly and is getting turned into anger?" It may be one emotion or many.

> An individual may be drawn to the adrenaline rush from blasting her anger.

Anger is an energy that seems to demand release. It acts like a heat-seeking missile looking for a target. It may create small to large outward explosions, ranging from irritated tone or biting sarcasm to rage. Or, it may implode, causing a drive to numb out, which may lead to depression or addictive behaviors.

There is some relief of pressure when anger is released, but it is short-lived. Pressure grows again and seeks another release opportunity. This cycle may be a driving force behind the abuse cycle: increasing tension leading to abuse incident(s) which are followed by a relief of tension and possibly apologies, but then tension increases again.

A woman may feel particularly justified in unleashing her anger if she thinks her man has done her wrong. She may feel culturally backed-up for throwing his things on the lawn, cutting up his clothes, or threatening to keep him from the children if she suspects he has transgressed her.

We seem to accept that "Hell has not fury like a woman scorned." We often give women a free pass, assuming they must be justified in whatever they feel and whatever action they take.

Self-defense

Self-defense is only *one* of the possible reasons
a woman might exhibit potentially abusive behaviors.

Many people minimize and discount the abuse of men by women through the claim that women only use potentially abusive behaviors in self-defense.

In reality, self-defense is only *one* of the possible reasons a woman might exhibit these behaviors. As I've shown, there are many other possible explanations.

> Self-defense would put potentially abusive behaviors on the *non-abusive* end of the continuum.

It is true that *sometimes* a woman will act in self-defense using behaviors that belong somewhere on the abuse continuum. Self-defense would put those behaviors on the *non-abusive* end of the continuum.

A woman might legitimately defend herself verbally, emotionally, financially, psychologically, physically, sexually, spiritually, or legally.

Ideally, a self-defensive move is a measured response befitting the situation and extinguishes the possibility of being harmed.

Sometimes there is an exaggerated self-defensive response to a situation. When a person feels threatened, her fight-or-flight response may be triggered. Unfortunately, the life-or-death response may be initiated by relatively minor or exaggerated "threats."

An individual may feel threatened by something that seems to be attacking her personality, opinion, or way of doing things. The threat may be as simple as her partner doesn't like eating pizza three days in a row. Even if he expresses himself with tact, she may still perceive it as a threat.

Sometimes a self-defensive move escalates the situation. In couples with poor communication skills, it is very common for verbal escalation to occur during arguments. If a message gets perceived as a threat, the person who feels threatened will make a decision whether to fight or flee. That decision may happen totally subconsciously as an instantaneous reaction.

Couples may become trapped in an escalation routine that looks like this (it could start with either "he" or "she"):

- she perceives a threat from him
- she escalates the situation
- he perceives a threat from her
- he escalates the situation
- and so on and so on

This attack-counterattack method of dealing with each other is non-productive at best and has the potential of being dangerous to the individuals and destructive to the relationship.

I want to reiterate: sometimes behaviors and attitudes that have the potential of being abusive are necessary for self-preservation. In those instances, the self-defensive behaviors would *not* be considered abusive.

Chapter 15

Physical reasons

When trying to figure out whether
a physical illness or condition
is the cause of abusive behavior,
it is important to check whether the
tendency for the behavior
existed before the illness or condition.

Hormonal challenges

We can't talk about abuse by women without addressing the issue of hormonal changes and challenges. Swings in hormone levels during pregnancy, monthly cycling, hormone treatments, illness, and menopause can alter mood and stimulate emotional overreactions.

> Inner-chemistry changes that accompany hormone adjustments may create edginess.

Inner-chemistry changes that accompany hormone adjustments may create edginess. Anxiety, depression, and irritability can all be influenced by those chemical changes.

There are many hormone changes with pregnancy. When these chemical changes are added to the many potential physical discomforts of carrying a growing and developing baby inside of her, the mother's mood may not be what she or others around her are used to. After giving birth, hormonal shifts may contribute to Postpartum Depression.

Many women who undergo hormone treatments for fertility or other reasons experience severe changes in mood. Cancers that impact a woman's centers of female hormone production (e.g., ovaries and breasts) mess with those hormone levels.

We often talk about the mood changes of PMS (Premenstrual Syndrome). Many women experience irritability as their menstrual period approaches. Renowned women's health specialist Christiane Northrup, M.D., characterizes the week around a woman's period as a time when the veils are thin between her and her emotions.

Emotions that a particular woman might be able to ignore during other phases of her menstrual cycle may be large and in charge during this time. If a woman doesn't do well with processing her uncomfortable emotions during the premenstrual and menstrual phases of her cycle, those uncomfortable emotions can show up as overreactions and anger.

From Dr. Northrup's perspective, women who haven't capitalized on the monthly opportunity to do an emotional house cleaning will be given the chance again in a big way with perimenopause* and menopause.** The major difference in the menopausal phase of life in this regard is that the emotion availability is constant rather than intermittent.

"At midlife, the hormonal milieu that was present for only a few days each month during most of your reproductive years, the milieu that was designed to spur you on to reexamine your life just a little at a time, now gets stuck in the on position for weeks or months at a time."[1]
—*The Wisdom of Menopause*, Christiane Northrup, M.D.

*Perimenopause is the flip side of adolescent hormone changes that occur as a girl's body revs up for making babies. With perimenopause, the hormones are adjusting away from fertility. Perimenopause may last from a few months to over ten years, but averages about four years.

**Natural menopause officially begins when it has been one year since a woman has had a menstrual period (as long as her periods haven't been altered by medication). Artificial menopause begins if a woman's ovaries are removed or are unable to function and she is not given replacement hormones.

Physical illness

It is difficult to be at our best when we are physically ill. We tend to feel tired and irritable when we are dragged down by an illness. In the short-term, it is relatively easy to overlook a partner's less-than-optimal attitudes and behaviors. Lethargy or a bad temper that is excused away because of illness may be more challenging to deal with and accept if the illness is extended or self-imposed.

Certain physical conditions may actually change a person's personality.

Dementia or Traumatic Brain Injury (TBI) may result in changes in mood that include anxiety, depression, irritability, and anger. There is hope that a person with TBI will improve as her injury heals. An individual with dementia is likely to continue to deteriorate as her illness progresses, but there are some techniques to try to limit her frustration and fear so that she is less likely to be reactionary.

When trying to figure out whether a physical illness is the cause of abusive behavior, it is important to check whether the tendency for the behavior existed before the illness.

Markers that a partner is using sickness as an excuse for abusive attitudes and actions include:

- the abuse is a "pre-existing condition" (existed before the illness),
- she doesn't really try to get well,
- she doesn't seek or follow reasonable medical advice, and/or
- she sabotages her health and makes her partner suffer the consequences.

Chapter 16

Mental health issues

Mental health issues such as anxiety and depression may be at the root of abusive behaviors and attitudes.

Overview

Mental illnesses and personality disorders are two different categories of mental/emotional conditions. Either may contribute to abusive behaviors and attitudes. Mental illnesses are associated with chemical imbalances and/or stimulating circumstances. Personality disorders are sets of traits that are integral to an individual's personality.

There may be overlap between and among mental illnesses and personality disorders. An individual may have more than one mental illness and/or personality disorder. (I'll talk more about personality disorders in the next chapter.)

Mental illnesses include such conditions as:

- depression,
- anxiety,
- posttraumatic stress, and
- bipolar disorders.

There is evidence that mental illnesses can be helped with medication and/or counseling. Bipolar disorders stand out in that an individual who is *properly diagnosed* with a bipolar disorder *needs* to take medication regularly in order to function well.

On the following pages, I list common signs and symptoms for several mental illnesses rather than the exact details of criteria used to officially diagnosis someone. This is meant to point out patterns of behaviors and attitudes to show how they may connect to partner abuse. (Full diagnostic criteria can be found in the *Diagnostic and Statistical Manual of Mental Disorders*.[1] Mental health professionals should be seen in person for an official diagnosis of mental illness.)

Depression

Depression is a set of symptoms that are sometimes rooted in a chemical imbalance; sometimes, the cause is more situational, psychological, or environmental.

Depressed thoughts, feelings, behaviors, and attitudes may be short-term or long-term. They may follow an event, such as the loss of a job, death of a loved one, or the birth of a child (Postpartum Depression); be stimulated by reduced sunshine (SAD, Seasonal Affective Disorder); or may be more omnipresent.

Many mental health professionals say that depression is anger turned inwards. As with anger, the question is: What emotional pain or discomfort is underneath it? What emotional discomfort isn't getting dealt with directly and is getting turned into depression? It may be one emotion. It may be many. The underlying emotions may be from recent events or from events long ago.

Depression can also be a learned way of being. A parent may model depressed behaviors and attitudes to their children. When those children grow into adults, they may carry with them a depressed approach to life.

There are varying degrees of depression. Each person's experience of depression can be placed on a continuum from not-at-all depressed to extreme depression:

totally happy	totally depressed

Feeling "somewhat down" could describe the quarter-way mark on the continuum. Symptoms that would place someone half-way along the continuum or beyond interfere with everyday life to a greater and greater degree. Being so depressed as to commit suicide is something that would be placed on the *totally depressed* end of the continuum.

Short-term depression connected to an event may impact the depressed person's partner negatively but at the same time be understandable and manageable. A man may feel more and more abused when his partner is depressed for an extended period of time and she is unwilling to address her depression.

> An individual may "enjoy" some payoff from hiding under the cover of depression.

A woman who isn't receptive to hearing about the impact that her longer-term depression has on her partner may "enjoy" some payoff from hiding under the cover of depression. Possible payoffs for depression include:

- getting out of work,
- being the center of attention,
- abdicating responsibility, or
- getting what she wants.

Possible signs and symptoms associated with depression include the following (not all are necessarily present in a depressed individual):

- feeling sad, unhappy, empty, hopeless, helpless, guilty, worthless, or self-loathing
- being emotionally numb
- being irritable or angry
- lacking in energy or motivation
- brain fog: difficulty thinking, concentrating, making decisions, or remembering things

- lack of interest in activities, especially in things that she would normally be interested in
- extreme pessimism
- overeating or disinterest in food
- insomnia, disturbed sleep, or excessive sleep
- physical aches and pains or digestive problems that don't respond to medical treatment
- suicidal thoughts, plans, or attempts (and in the worst case, suicide completion)

A depressed woman's depression can wear her partner out. Her depression is particularly destructive to a relationship if she:

- doesn't want to participate in life,
- extracts a cost from her partner for any fun he wants to have,
- makes him responsible for her mood,
- drags down the whole household's energy,
- hates seeing other people be happy,
- makes her partner carry more than a fair share of responsibility for an extended period of time,
- is disinterested in sex (especially if she shames him for having a normal level of interest),
- shows him little or no affection,
- is not really a partner or companion,
- is attacking and blaming,
- uses suicidal threats as manipulation,
- is attached to her depression, or
- doesn't take reasonable steps to try to get better.

Anxiety and stress

Anxiety is a heightened state of fear. It is usually created through ongoing exposure to something scary or by tapping into a reservoir of stored fear. The stored fear may be from one particular experience that has become stuck, or it may be an accumulation from many scary experiences. Anxiety is often labeled as *stress*.

> Anxiety is a heightened state of fear. It is often labeled as *stress*.

The message in fear is "danger." The danger may be real, exaggerated, or imagined. It may be physical, psychological, emotional, financial, legal, sexual, or spiritual.

Anxiety may stem from fear of:

- physical danger,
- betrayal,
- loss,
- abandonment,
- rejection,
- failure,
- success,
- crowds,
- roads,
- change,
- not being able to get everything done,
- imperfection,
- public speaking,
- not making the mortgage payment,
- losing control, or
- almost anything, depending on the individual's history, experiences, and coping ability.

When the level of fear experienced is warranted by the situation, that fear helps people respond to the threat. It helps them keep themselves and others safe. When the level of fear experienced is an overreaction to current circumstances, instead of offering protection, it can get in the way of health and happiness.

People who are experiencing overreactions of fear may get anxious just at the thought of exposure to a feared thing, or the imagined possibility of a feared thing happening.

Anxiety can:

- create overreactions,
- morph into the secondary emotion of anger,
- be debilitating,
- inhibit achievement,
- drive obsessions or compulsions,
- be expressed as demands,
- galvanize rigidity,
- activate withdrawal,
- use up patience (both theirs and yours), or
- stimulate fear of fear.

Anxiety tends to take over the brain making it spin replaying awfulized, exaggerated worst-case scenarios that are worse than realistic, rational worst-case scenarios.

We have the same emotional reaction to something vividly imagined as we do with something that actually happens, so vividly imagining something scary over and over creates a growing mushroom cloud of fear. A partner may be blindsided when that overdeveloped fear is expressed as accusations, demands, withdrawal, rage, or other challenging attitudes and behaviors.

Posttraumatic stress

Posttraumatic stress is a stuck response to trauma. The person re-experiences the trauma of terrible events from her past. It is a pattern of behaviors and overwhelming thoughts and feelings that result from experiencing or witnessing a life-threatening traumatic event or series of events directly or indirectly. The official disorder is known as PTSD.

Direct exposure to a traumatic event occurs when an individual experiences or witnesses a shocking or violent life-threatening situation herself. Indirect exposure occurs if her loved one has a violent or accidental life-threatening event, or if her job (e.g., police officer) repeatedly exposes her to tragic circumstances of others.

People suffering from posttraumatic stress may be irritable, angry, overreactive, or aggressive. They may have anxiety and/or depression. They may express a persistently negative view of themselves, other people, or the world in general.

Medication and therapy have both been shown to help posttraumatic stress.

Signs and symptoms associated with posttraumatic stress cover four categories (not all the signs and symptoms are necessarily present in an individual).

1. Intrusive thoughts about the traumatic event(s), such as:

    -   flashbacks
    -   nightmares
    -   extreme physical or emotional reactions to events that remind her of the trauma

2. Avoidance of things associated with the traumatic event(s):

- trying to avoid thoughts and feelings connected to the event(s)
- trying to avoid things or people that remind her of the event(s)

3. Altered ability to think about the event(s) or associated mood, for example having any or all of:

- memory blanks regarding the event(s)
- exaggerated negative views of herself, others, or the world in general (absolutes such as "I can't trust anyone")
- distorted beliefs about the event's cause
- anxiety
- extreme guilt or shame
- depression

4. Feeling "on edge," possibly including being:

- irritable
- overly angry
- verbally or physically aggressive
- reckless
- self-destructive
- hypervigilant
- easily startled
- unable to sleep well
- unable to concentrate

Posttraumatic stress has a ripple effect on families. Severe PTSD can put the sufferer's partner in extreme danger if stress stimulates a violent automatic response.

Bipolar disorders

There are several official diagnoses that fall on the bipolar spectrum. People with bipolar disorders experience the polar-opposite low and high states of depression and mania. When they are unmedicated, they typically swing between the two poles.

Bipolar mood swings might be quick and often, or a person properly diagnosed may only have experienced one period of mania with a long pattern of depression. It is also possible for both manic and depressed symptoms to appear at the same time or be "mixed" together.

Mania is a hyper state. It is often characterized by days of not needing or wanting much sleep. (This is not the same as being unable to sleep because of anxiety or staying up to cram for an exam.) Someone with a bipolar disorder may experience long full-blown manic periods or milder "hypomanic" symptoms.

People often have grandiose thinking during a manic phase. They may start business ventures while manic only to have them crash and burn when they come down from the mania.

> An individual may be very impulsive during a manic episode.

Mania may lead to impulsive behaviors, such as promiscuity, gambling, or excessive spending. An individual may enjoy the high feeling they get when they are manic.

Psychosis can be part of the bipolar package. Psychosis is a break from reality. It can hit in either a severely depressed or severely manic phase of the illness. It can include delusions (strongly held illogical beliefs) or hallucinations (seeing, smelling, or hearing things that aren't there).

If there are delusions in a manic phase, there is a tendency toward delusions of grandeur. In a depressed phase, delusions are more oppressive and paranoid (e.g., believing they are being followed or watched, or people are plotting against them).

The potential symptoms of bipolar depression are the same as those described in the depression section a few pages back.

Potential manic signs and symptoms include the following (not all are necessarily present in a manic individual):

- extreme energy
- lack of sleepiness
- euphoric "high" feeling
- increased irritability (potentially leading to rage)
- increased talkativeness
- physical agitation or restlessness
- overconfidence
- inflated sense of self
- grandiose ideas
- increased sex drive
- risk taking
- heightened creativity
- hyperfocused on a goal or multiple goals
- poor judgment
- racing thoughts
- rapid speech
- easily distracted
- flying from one idea to another

The distorted thinking of mania may cause an individual to:

- be totally blind to the fact that they need help;
- quickly flip from euphoria to anger;
- dangerously use drugs or alcohol;
- be sexually promiscuous;
- behave aggressively;
- intrude into other people's lives;
- obsessively text, email, or phone;
- go on spending sprees;
- gamble;
- give away possessions;
- make risky investments;
- rack up debt;
- blow off work, school, or other responsibilities;
- drive recklessly; and/or
- initiate grandiose plans that can't be sustained.

The good news with bipolar disorders is that medication is usually extremely helpful. It may take some experimentation to figure out what particular mix of medications is ideal for a particular person, but many people have a high degree of symptom relief with medication.

Once the medication regimen that works for an individual is discovered, they *must* take it religiously and not mix it with mind-altering substances. Sometimes medications need to be adjusted because of changes in the individual's circumstances (e.g., new stressors) or environment (e.g., seasonal changes).

Relapsing because they stop taking their medication when they feel better is a huge problem among people with bipolar disorders and other types of mental illness.

Addictions and substance abuse

For an addicted person, nothing is as important as getting and using their substance. You can't compete with an addicted partner's substance of choice. She will lie about whether she is using, where she is, where she's going, and what she's doing. She is irritable when she is craving a fix. She is defensive when you attempt to talk about her addiction.

> It may seem like your addicted partner doesn't love you, but really, she just loves her "substance" more.

When a person is addicted, the chemical change experienced when using her substance of choice draws her back over and over, even though the behavior has a negative impact on her life. People can become addicted to, or abuse the consumption of, just about anything:

- drugs or alcohol
- tobacco
- sex
- sugar, caffeine, or food in general
- bingeing and purging
- gambling
- shopping
- exercise, tanning, or plastic surgery
- anger

The mind-altering aspect of drugs and alcohol can change a person's personality, intensify emotions, magnify shortcomings, or remove their inhibitions. For example, a drunk person may be belligerent, volatile, and aggressive; or, on the other extreme, the alcohol may cause her to be mentally absent, nonsensical, and lethargic. A drunk person's behavior may fall somewhere between these two extremes but still be destructive to relationships. She may make really bad choices, like being unfaithful.

An individual may abuse a particular substance but not be addicted to it. For example, someone might abuse alcohol but not be an alcoholic. A hierarchy of alcohol use can be viewed as:

1. Abstinence: doesn't use alcohol at all (she doesn't want to or is in recovery from addiction)
2. Healthy use: uses alcohol with total control over when and how much; it doesn't have a negative impact on health, relationships, work, etc.
3. Abuses the substance: doesn't control consumption well; there is a negative impact from the amount of use sometimes or often
4. Addiction: compelled to consume alcohol at unhealthy levels; there is a negative impact from the amount of use sometimes or often

For someone addicted to a drug or alcohol, it is usually an all-or-nothing proposition. They can't consume some without consuming too much.

Someone who abuses a substance but is not addicted may be able to learn to use the substance in a healthy way. Some substances are so physically addictive that there is no middle ground. Someone who has had a problem with heroin can't have any without getting into trouble again.

Most people need help to get over addictions. They need to acknowledge they have a problem, figure out what drew them to the destructive choices, change their habits, develop new healthy coping skills, and, in many cases, find a source of ongoing support.

Chapter 17

Personality disorders

People with these personality disorders
are driven to have their own needs met.
They are so obsessed with that singular goal
that they have grave difficulty offering the give and take
necessary for healthy relationships.

Overview

The signs and symptoms of personality disorders are more pervasive than those seen with mental illnesses. The pattern of behaviors and attitudes exhibited by individuals with personality disorders is actually part of their personality.

There are many personality disorders that are relevant to a discussion of why women abuse men, including:

- narcissistic,
- borderline,
- dependent,
- histrionic,
- sociopathic, and
- dependent personalities.

> Many of the signs and symptoms for the various personality disorders are described by words such as *extreme*, *excessive*, or *intense*.

There is quite a bit of crossover between various personality disorders. An individual may have more than one personality disorder, and may have both a personality disorder and a mental illness (such as depression or anxiety).

Many of the signs and symptoms for the various personalities are described by words such as *extreme*, *excessive*, or *intense*. The behaviors and attitudes of people with personality disorders are found in healthy people, but with personality disorders the behaviors and attitudes are exaggerated versions.

People with these personalities are driven to have their own needs met. They are so obsessed with that singular goal that they have grave difficulty offering the give and take necessary for healthy relationships.

They are typically attached to being the way that they are, not open to acknowledging that they have destructive behaviors and attitudes, and likely to be very defensive if confronted about their behavior.

Medications may help with aspects of what they have going on, such as depression or anxiety, but many of their traits are not helped by medication. Short-term counseling is of little help. There is some hope of change for *self-motivated* people in very *specialized long-term* therapy programs.

If a woman with a personality disorder genuinely wants to change, she must be in it for the long haul. It takes a great deal of commitment, time, and focus to make lasting personality changes.

On the following pages, I present the clusters of traits generally associated with each personality type. It can be helpful to see if someone stressful to you has a grouping of behaviors and attitudes that are shared by other people.

(Full diagnostic criteria for personality disorders can be found in the *Diagnostic and Statistical Manual of Mental Disorders.*[1] Mental health professionals should be seen in person for an official diagnosis.)

Narcissistic personality

Narcissists see themselves as high achieving, independent of whether or not they are high achieving. From their perspective, they are the most important person in the room. They are arrogant and angered by anyone that they perceive to not be catering to their spoken or unspoken "needs."

The signs and symptoms of narcissistic personality include the following (not all are necessarily present in an individual):

- self-centered
- grandiose
- extreme arrogance
- needs admiration
- attitude of entitlement
- lacks empathy
- exaggerates her achievements and talents
- fantasizes about extreme power, success, beauty. . .

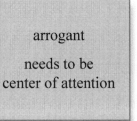

arrogant

needs to be center of attention

- doesn't care about other people's thoughts and feelings (although she might appear to care if it serves her in some way)
- can't stand criticism
- exploits others
- envious of others
- thinks other people envy her
- expects to be treated as special
- wants to associate only with people she considers to have high status
- takes advantage of people
- becomes angry if she feels she has not been properly attended to

Drew Keys founded the website LightsHouse.org for adult children of toxic parents. He writes extensively about narcissists. He has also published the book *Narcissists Exposed: 75 Things Narcissists Don't Want You to Know*.

Keys says:

"When narcissists are nice, they are virtually always doing it for something they want, or because it benefits THEM to do so. Don't make the mistake of thinking that someone who does nice things cannot be narcissistic. It's not at all true; in fact, a significant percentage of narcissists enjoy playing saint. In addition, even very toxic people can be nice, at least on occasion."[2]

"When do narcissists cry? Narcissists cry for themselves. Because they lack empathy, when they cry, they are crying for what they personally wanted and didn't get, for the upset, loss, or disappointment they feel, or to get your pity so you'll do more for them and give them more attention, more support, and more leniency."[3]

> "When do narcissists cry? Narcissists cry for themselves."
> —Drew Keys

A narcissist may draw a partner by her stories of how great she is. She may even be high achieving. She may be beautiful. It may take some time for the partner to question the validity of her stories and recognize her exaggerations.

A narcissist's partner will often tire of being criticized for not taking care of the narcissist in ways she wants to be taken care of, while none of his needs are worthy of her consideration.

Borderline personality

The term *borderline* was first used to describe a set of personality traits that bordered between neurotic (mental distress) and psychotic (break from reality). That set of traits is included in what is now known in North America as Borderline Personality Disorder (BPD).

People with borderline personality tend to run hot and cold. They love you or they hate you. They go through a lot of relationships, both romantic and platonic. They wear partners and friends out. Relationships that do last for them are usually with partners who are particularly perseverant.

The word, or concept of, *unstable* crops up a lot when describing people with borderline personality. They have unstable emotions, unstable image of themselves, unstable relationships, and impulsive destructive behavior. In fact, the international title for BPD is Emotionally Unstable Personality Disorder. (North America is moving towards adopting the international system for mental health designations.)

unstable: emotions, self-image, and relationships

The signs and symptoms of borderline personality include the following (not all are necessarily present in an individual):

- unstable relationships
- extreme fear of abandonment
- separation anxiety when away from her loved ones
- viewing people as absolutely wonderful or absolutely terrible
- quickly flipping her assessment of a person from wonderful to terrible or vice versa

- unstable self-image
- chameleon-like: lacking a clear sense of self, she may take on the opinions and behaviors of others as her own
- very intense emotions
- very overreactive
- extreme mood swings (short-lived episodes of depression, irritability, anxiety, anger . . .)
- verbally and/or physically abusive
- feeling empty and worthless
- severe dissociation, numbness, or detachment
- anger, rage, aggression
- paranoia
- recklessly impulsive with spending, shoplifting, dangerous driving, substance abuse, bingeing and purging, risky sexual behavior . . .
- self-mutilation such as cutting or burning herself*
- suicidal gestures, threats, or completion
- lacking in boundaries
- controlling
- manipulative
- sees herself as right and others as wrong

The borderline person's fear of abandonment may result in her reacting in extreme ways to anything that triggers her feelings of abandonment. Her partner being a few minutes late can set off rage or tears. She may lash out at a friend for cancelling a lunch meeting, or threaten suicide if she suspects that her partner is considering ending their relationship.

*While self-harm such as superficially cutting on arms and legs is very typical borderline personality behavior, it is *not* necessarily present in every person with BPD, and every person who "cuts" does *not* necessarily have BPD.

Histrionic personality

Histrionic personalities are flamboyant, melodramatic attention-seekers. The root of the word *histrionic* is the same as that of *hysterical*. A histrionic woman may be the life of the party and draw a partner in with her enthusiasm, charm, and seduction, but then wear him out with her need to be the center of the universe.

The signs and symptoms of histrionic personality include the following (not all are necessarily present in an individual):

- dramatic
- over-the-top emotions
- overly enthusiastic
- rapidly flipping emotions
- craves being the center of attention
- feels put out if not the center of attention
- uses physical appearance to get attention
- envious of others who get attention
- flirtatious
- seductive
- excessive need for approval
- overly sensitive to criticism
- self-indulgent
- self-centered
- tends to think relationships are more intimate than they really are
- easily influenced by other people
- manipulative
- willing to lie and make up stories to get attention

melodramatic

attention-seeking

seductive

- overspends on physical "trappings" (clothes, makeup . . .)
- blames others for her shortcomings and disappointments
- expresses strong, passionate opinions that she can't back up with detail or reason
- has trouble with delaying gratification: wants gratification right now
- uses suicide threats to gain attention and manipulate

Like women with borderline personality (BPD), histrionic women may threaten suicide; however, there is a major difference regarding suicide between the two personalities. While 8–10% of people with BPD complete suicides, completed suicides among people with Histrionic Personality Disorder is much less characteristic.[4]

Drew Keys describes histrionic personality at LightsHouse.org:

"Talking is one of the easiest ways to capture and maintain people's attention, and histrionic people love attention, so excessive talking is often seen in people with Histrionic Personality Disorder (HPD) traits.

The two most highly-favored topics are themselves and their current drama; however, if that fails to gain attention, whatever topic works will be used.

HPD people are often (but not always) very gregarious and chatty, and frequently interrupt and dominate conversations, having little patience for topics not central to their reality."

Sociopathic personality

Sociopaths are parasites. Like other parasitic creatures, sociopaths need a "host" for survival. They are on the lookout for strong, healthy hosts. When they find a suitable host, they latch on, and aren't satisfied until they have sucked the life out of the person who has had the misfortune of becoming their target.

> Sociopaths are parasites. They latch on to people and suck the life out of them.

When we think of sociopathic partners, we most often think of those that kill. But sociopathy can be put on a continuum from zero to Jodi Arias. On this continuum, everyone past the half-way mark is going to cause problems for people who come in contact with them. As you move along the continuum of sociopathic behavior, the perpetrators become more and more destructive.

Some sociopaths (such as Jodi Arias or Scott Peterson) physically kill their targets. Others kill their psyche, financial health, self-esteem, reputation, ability to have another relationship, or their spirit.

The diagnostic manual used by mental health professionals uses the term Antisocial Personality Disorder to designate a pattern of attitudes and behaviors we commonly call psychopathy or sociopathy.[5]

Being without conscience and enjoying lying are two key elements of sociopathic personality. These elements go hand in hand in that sociopaths' lack of conscience means that they can lie without showing the normal markers of lying. That's how they pull people into believing their lies and get away with as much as they get away with. They are so practiced at lying that they respond to being caught in a lie by creating a new lie. It is very difficult to pin them down. Their lies tend to be complex and detailed.

Sociopaths don't care about collateral damage: they don't care who or what gets hurt by their actions and attitudes. They get focused on their goal and can see nothing else. They don't care if it hurts their children. They will often even put themselves in danger because of their laser focus on whatever goal they have at the time.

The signs and symptoms of sociopathic personality include the following (not all are necessarily present in an individual):

- little or no conscience
- irritable and aggressive
- can be charming
- uses people
- impulsive
- enjoys lying
- lies without conscience (therefore, she doesn't show the normal markers of lying)
- extremely self-centered and self-serving
- can bring up crocodile tears (fake crying used to give the illusion of sadness, remorse, hurt . . .)
- lacks remorse: doesn't offer *genuine* apologies
- cannot feel empathy for others
- doesn't think rules and laws are for her
- doesn't care about collateral damage when she is trying to achieve her self-centered goals
- extremely manipulative
- malicious: loves a cat-and-mouse game of toying with her target

manipulative

self-centered

lies without conscience

- doesn't plan ahead (except for her immediate plotting and scheming)
- irresponsible
- can be high achieving (usually by using others)
- can be low achieving and expect other people to take care of her
- has contempt for kind, "good" people
- vengeful
- feels no gratitude for what others do for her
- presents different versions of herself to different audiences depending on her performance goals
- loves to take from other people (beauty, achievement, strength, money, self-esteem . . .)
- extracts people's sympathy

According to Martha Stout, author of *The Sociopath Next Door*, 4% of the population is sociopathic.[6] That is 1 in 25. We bump up against sociopaths in our neighborhoods, workplaces, and grocery stores. Those of us who are particularly unlucky partner with one.

To snare targeted partners, sociopaths often play the "poor me, I've been done wrong by another man," sympathy-grabbing card; and/or pour on the charm. Some call sociopaths' charm trapping technique "love bombing": lavishing compliments and demonstrations of their appreciation, becoming the person that they have figured out their target wants to be with, and acting out the part of an ideal sexual partner.

When you try to get out of a relationship with a sociopath, and sometimes even when she calls it quits and moves on to a new target, instead of love bombing there often is all-out war. The parasite is thirsty for nourishment. Tearing other people down feeds and builds up the sociopath.

Dependent personality

On the flip side of loud, aggressive abuse is quiet, draining abuse that grows out of excessive dependence. A person with dependent personality has extreme difficulty functioning as an equal partner. She needs to be taken care of. Her helplessness exerts control over her partner.

The signs and symptoms of dependent personality include the following (not all are necessarily present in an individual):

- uncomfortable being alone
- craves support and nurturing
- requires constant reassurance
- helpless
- submissive
- clingy
- pessimistic
- needs to be taken care of
- excessively seeks advice even for minor decisions
- extracts the help of others
- extreme self-doubt and self-criticism
- fears separation and abandonment
- difficulty making decisions
- difficulty doing things on her own
- can't take responsibility for her own welfare
- difficulty expressing her own opinions

> extreme need to be taken care of

A man may be drawn into a new relationship with a dependent personality because he thinks he can help this Damsel in Distress. He may eventually become worn out by her never-ending need to be carried and realize that no amount of effort on his part helps her become psychologically stronger.

Part Four

Men who are abused

How men get pulled in

Abusive people do a sales job on their targets.
They get them to buy in to a relationship with them and
then continue to sell them on living with their requirements.

In the beginning

It's easy enough to see why mildly abusive relationships keep going: abuse may be a relatively small part of the relationship. It may be challenging to understand how more severely abusive relationships make it past a first date.

A major factor that contributes to a man being drawn into a relationship with an abusive woman is that he simply doesn't expect it. Lack of discussion about the phenomenon of women abusing men sets men up to be blindsided.

Many men who find themselves in the position of being the target of partner abuse didn't see it coming. Possibly:

- the relationship started out well and then went sour;
- the markers of an abusive nature were present early but went unrecognized;
- the woman initially camouflaged her true self; or
- the man recognized the abusive behaviors/attitudes of his new partner but chose to look past them.

A man may be pulled towards a woman who is in need of rescue. Helping a Damsel in Distress may seem like the manly thing to do. Fulfilling the role of saving a woman who has been wronged by other men (or so she says) can be particularly heady. A man may endure a lot of pain in order to rehabilitate the image of his gender.

The abundant hormone exchange of a new, exciting relationship can be intoxicating. There is good reason for the common phrase "Love is blind." The feel-good chemicals stimulated by intense love and sex make the draw to the object of affection (and/or source of orgasms) very great. The danger red flags might be there, but they are rendered invisible by the hormonal haze.

Possible reasons why a man might be pulled into a relationship that is on the higher end of the abuse continuum include that he is:

- abusive himself (sometimes abuse is mutual);
- blinded by love;
- blinded by the sex;
- desperate to be in a relationship;
- attached to her positive qualities;
- a nice guy who wants to prove that guys can be considerate, flexible, dependable, nurturing . . .;
- in denial about the red flags of danger;
- convinced she needs him; or
- too quick to commit.

It may be that he:

- witnessed his parents abuse each other,
- was abused as a child,
- thinks the abusive behavior or attitudes are just the way women are,
- has a distorted idea of what love looks like,
- was raised in a healthy household and doesn't recognize abuse,
- doesn't realize the potential of women being abusive because of the lack of cultural conversation around the topic,
- wants to help a Damsel in Distress,
- commits because she is pregnant,
- thinks her bad behavior must be his fault,
- enjoys her attention,
- falls for Dating Girl, or
- becomes "sold" on the idea of the relationship.

Dating Girl

Sometimes the abuse red flags are minimized or absent at the beginning of relationships because the participant(s) temporarily mask their real personality. People often become what I call *Dating Guy* and *Dating Girl* while courting a potential partner. They put on a personality they think will be well received.

This may be an innocent and/or subconscious attempt to put one's best foot forward. It may be part of a malicious plan to purposefully deceive and entrap. It may be something in between.

Dating Guy and Dating Girl personalities may be close to the real thing or far from reality. Many a man has fallen in love with a woman's

> Dating Girl may reappear after a breakup (threatened or actual) or whenever a woman is trying to woo her man, then disappear once again after he's committed to her.

dating personality and then become confused when that personality is replaced by an evil alter ego.

When the Dating Girl personality disappears, her partner may assume he must be inadequate or wrong in some way and that it's his fault she is now demeaning, controlling, or punishing. He may desperately try to figure out what he can do to get that great, happy, loving woman to reappear. But there may be no way back to that personality, because it was just a temporary facade.

One couple went to several different counselors in attempts to salvage their relationship. Actually, a better description would be that they went to several different counselors in the woman's attempts to find one that would talk her boyfriend into giving in to her many demands.

The boyfriend struggled desperately to figure out how to be a good partner without abandoning his wants and needs entirely. He was absolutely convinced that if he was good enough the qualities his girlfriend demonstrated the first several months of their relationship would return.

In reality, the girlfriend's demanding/controlling persona that ramped up a few months into the relationship was the real deal.

He was in love with Dating Girl, not Commitment Girl. Dating Girl would only temporarily reappear to hook him back in when he gave up on the relationship. (*Commitment Girl* denotes that a man has made a commitment to her. It is not indicative of her making a commitment to him.)

Presenting a temporary artificial dating personality which is intended to get a potential partner to commit to a relationship is a classic bait-and-switch maneuver.

Note: The subconscious phenomenon known as *confirmation bias* helps explain why some men get stuck thinking that their partner's Dating Girl personality must be the "real" her even when she breaks from the facade.

Confirmation bias is the tendency for a person to notice and take in that which confirms what they already believe to be true, and ignore evidence that contradicts what they believe.

Once a man believes a particular woman to be considerate, rational, and loving, confirmation bias gets in the way of him noticing evidence to the contrary.

The sales job

After hearing many people's stories about the abuse they experienced in relationships, and thinking about how it was that I became entangled with a man that abused me, I recognized that sales techniques are often used by abusive people to sell potential partners on the relationship.

These same sales techniques may be used again during the relationship to secure buy-in from the partner.

It is possible that a particular woman might use the sales approach subconsciously and innocently to promote herself in an honest way. In that case, she genuinely is who she presents herself to be and her intention is to help a partner see how well they fit together.

Another woman might use the sales approach consciously and maliciously to deceive and entrap. I'm not saying she necessarily knows the academic theory behind what she's doing; she may just have found through trial and error what gets the job done.

Various sales gurus promote a multiple-stage sales cycle. The number of stages/steps each describes varies, but the basic concepts are similar across the board.

The basic sales cycle includes several steps:

1. Prospecting
2. Establish rapport
3. Qualify the prospective buyer
4. Prepare and package the presentation
5. Manage objections
6. Close the sale
7. Service after the sale

1. Prospecting

Selling All-in-One for Dummies describes the goal of prospecting as "finding the right potential buyer for what you're selling."[1]

The elements of prospecting for buyers include defining the target market and attracting potential buyers.

A woman may test the waters with many men before finding one who she can get to do what she wants him to do and lets her get away with what she wants to get away with.

The target market for a particular woman depends on her particular needs. If she is healthy, she'll be looking for a healthy partner. If she is dependent, she is looking for a man who will take care of her. If she is manipulative, she wants a man she can manipulate. If she is angry, she is prospecting for a man she can yell at, or hit, or put down.

This quote from *Selling All-in-One for Dummies* is relevant for attracting a potential partner: "To persuade another person to give you his valuable time, you need to offer something of value in return."[2]

A woman may use attention, cooking, money, conversation, flattery, or sex to "offer something of value." A beautiful woman's valuable offering to a man might simply be her presence. He might be drawn to her just to be with a pretty woman.

Women who are very abusive thrive when they have someone to abuse. When one relationship ends, or just before it ends, they will go into a prospecting frenzy to quickly find another target to abuse.

2. Establish rapport

Establishing rapport is about creating a strong connection. It involves making the other person think the two of you are similar. In a healthy, honest relationship, rapport automatically grows through recognition of common interests, views, goals, and ways of being. But rapport can be artificially created when those commonalities are absent or limited, or when someone wants to hide their true nature.

A number of mechanisms for building rapport surface in sales training materials:

- flattery
- friendship
- empathy
- commonality

> The master of influence, Tony Robbins, says: "Rapport is the ability to enter someone else's world, to make him feel that you understand him, that you have a strong common bond."

Flattery

Studies show that flattery is a particularly potent tool for building rapport. The person receiving the compliment automatically creates a positive view of the person offering the compliment. In his article "4 Common Sales Techniques People Fall For," Ben DeMeter says, "the most commonly used technique in any sales representative's arsenal of tactics is flattery."[3]

Friendship

Abraham Lincoln said: "If you would win a man to your cause, first convince him that you are his sincere friend." The other mechanisms for building rapport are ways to convince someone you are his friend.

Empathy

Empathy is the ability to identify with other people's feelings and circumstances. A woman who fakes empathy will create the illusion that she understands and cares about her target.

Commonality

Commonality builds bonds. We are drawn to people who are similar to us. This is especially true when looking for a life partner. We want someone who will support our goals and aspirations, and make our life better.

A woman may fake commonalities by seeming to be interested in what a potential partner is interested in, pretending to like the things he likes, or by tailoring her personality to suit his. She may pretend to respect his view of the world.

Establishing a common enemy is a particularly powerful rapport builder. It creates a "you and me against the world" mindset. It isolates the couple and fosters dependence on the partner.

When a woman complains about her horrible ex-partners, those exes become the shared enemy of her and her new partner. It throws the new partner into Protector Mode.

Being in Protector Mode decreases a man's receptivity to any information that might be damaging to the image of the woman he is defending. He will be less able to see red flags when they appear and less open to any negative comments his friends and family might have about the woman.

The bonding effect of having a common enemy is explained in psychology by the concept of triangulation. Triangulation gives a false sense of closeness.

Triangulation of a couple and common enemy looks like this:

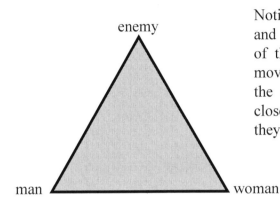

Notice how far apart the man and woman are at the bottom of the triangle. As they each move up the triangle towards the enemy, the sides become closer and closer together until they meet and become one.

Many different people, things, or situations can be triangulated into a couple:

- her "terrible" boss or ex
- health concerns
- drugs or alcohol
- children

When you are both focused on the same thing, it feels like you are close to each other.

A woman might use her children from a previous relationship to build commonality with a new partner. If she can get him to care about her children, the new couple now has a third point (the children) to give the feeling of closeness.

3. Qualify the prospective buyer

Again, from *Selling All-in-One for Dummies*: "In selling, *qualifying* your prospects means finding out not just who they are but also what they do, what they have, and what they need in order to confirm that your product or service is a good fit and that they have the resources to invest in it."[4]

In a new relationship with healthy potential, this sales step would equate to a woman checking out a man to see if they are a good fit for each other, and deciphering whether a relationship would be mutually beneficial.

If an individual's "product or service" is abuse, then she may look to qualify a potential partner by determining whether he will be a good fit for her abusive ways. She may test him. She may do this on purpose, or it may be automatically built in to any potential relationship with her.

The tests will likely start out small and subtle. If he passes the test, he'll stick around and she'll continue to build a relationship with him, potentially creating more tests. If he passes the tests—he loses.

If the tests expose that she thinks and behaves in ways that are unacceptable to a particular man, then he may decide to drop the relationship, or she may make adjustments to her approach so she can keep him long enough to get a commitment from him.

Some women don't risk the exposure of their real personality that testing would entail, but instead keep the Dating Girl facade tightly in place. They use the qualifying round just to determine whether a particular man has enough of what they want: enough money, enough love, enough naiveté, status, perseverance, determination . . .

4. Prepare and package the presentation

Like with product commercials, this is the stage when a woman highlights what she guesses the potential partner will be attracted to (physically and otherwise) and minimizes or camouflages detrimental information.

She may use a hard-sell or soft-sell presentation to get a man to buy in to a relationship. Hard selling is direct, high pressure, insistent, and overt. The soft-sell approach is subtle, suggestive, indirect, and persuasive.

We should probably add a third category for the Dating Girl version of a woman who is purposefully hiding her true self from view until the sale is closed: the magic-sell. (Now you see it, now you don't. Poof, Dating Girl's gone.)

Malicious-woman relationship sales techniques include:

- sex,
- glory,
- martyrdom, and
- obligation through reciprocity.

Sex

We all know sex sells. Sex sells cars and widgets. And sex can be used to sell a man on a relationship.

Glory

A woman might frequently recount how wonderful she is to try and convince her partner she's a great catch.

During his divorce from an abusive woman, one man remembered that while they were dating, "She was always giving me her résumé." She was always talking about her accomplishments and describing herself in glowing terms.

After they were married, he noticed discrepancies between her description of herself and reality, but it was too late. He had trained himself to ignore those discrepancies. It was only after his divorce that he had the time and space to fully accept that she had sold him a bill of goods.

Martyrdom

When I was doing Internet research about sales techniques, I came across advice for sales reps to "make them think you're a martyr."[5] It seems to perfectly describe what some women do to pull in a man. The package presentation is: "Woe is me. I've been done wrong. You need to help me."

Obligation through reciprocity

One of Ben DeMeter's 4 Common Sales Techniques People Fall For is "Obligation through reciprocity." He describes the power of playing on a target buyer's sense of obligation and feelings of guilt. "People naturally have a sense of reciprocity that leads them to believe that after something nice is done for them, they should do something nice for the benevolent party in return."[6]

This means that a woman who is manipulative instead of "benevolent" can use a man's natural inclination toward reciprocity to keep him attached to, and doing for, her. He ends up doing a lot more for her than she does for him:

- she gives attention, he gives his life;
- she gives gifts, he gives his life;
- she gives sex, he gives his life . . .

5. Manage objections

During the managing objections stage, the promoter tries to figure out what objections her target has to committing to the product (in this case a relationship or whatever the woman wants) and extinguishes those objections.

Some sales trainers call this step "Inoculate against objection." That title feels particularly creepy to me. To inoculate someone against an idea or feeling denotes a permanent immunity or resistance. The objection may be a healthy one. The objection may be there to protect and defend. Inoculation would render the objection permanently powerless to do its job.

One man recounted that his former partner, who pulled the rug out from under him by ending their relationship shortly after he sold his home and furnishings, quit his job, and moved to be with her, had very convincingly told him: "I'll never hurt you." She realized while they were dating that he was afraid of being hurt again (his objection) and she managed that objection with her reassuring and emphatic statement that she would never hurt him.

An individual might use the *foot in the door* technique to handle objections. This approach takes advantage of the theory that someone is more likely to say yes to a small request rather than a large one, and that bigger yeses can be solicited if the size of the request grows incrementally rather than jumps to full size immediately. Smaller yeses lead to bigger yeses. For example, a man who would likely say no to a request

> The *foot in the door* technique for managing objections: small yeses lead to bigger yeses

for a "loan" of $1,000, may eventually part with the whole sum through a series of requests for more modest, but increasingly large, amounts of money.

One salesman talked about leaving his coat behind when he went on a sales call that didn't end with a purchase order. It gave him a chance to return and address the target buyer's concerns or objections. I call this the *leave something behind* technique.

> Building up a stash of personal belongings at a boyfriend's home is a combination of two techniques to manage objections: *leave something behind* and *foot in the door.*

The relationship tactic of leaving growing numbers of personal items at a dating partner's home reminds me of both the *leave something behind* and the *foot in the door* sales techniques. Leaving the belongings behind becomes part of a slow, incremental moving-in process. Before the partner knows it, they're living together.

If there is a threat that the relationship may end, a woman may use gold-medal-level flattery: "You are so wonderful; I can't live without you." This may come in the form of a sad-puppy-dog look of dismay that pulls on the partner's heartstrings. It may come in the form of a feigned suicide attempt.

The "You are so wonderful; I can't live without you" message has the potential of serving as a catch-all objection killer, rendering all his thoughts of ending the relationship lifeless.

6. Close the sale

This is the step when the promoter gets their target to make a commitment.

Salespeople know that if a potential buyer leaves the building or hangs up the phone, there is reduced likelihood of closing the sale. They don't want to give the buyer the space and time to clear their head. They want them focused on the product and their persuasions.

Capitalizing on a partner's time with text messages, phone calls, and dates makes him easier to persuade. Also, isolation from friends and family may help a woman close the sale, because it limits outside influences that might raise objections.

> An accidental-on-purpose pregnancy is the ultimate relationship deal closer.

Future pacing may be part of closing tactics. Future pacing is accomplished by engaging the target in graphic fantasy of how wonderful they are going to feel after the purchase. If a company is selling cars, future pacing involves helping you see how great life would be in that car. If a woman is using future pacing to sell you on a relationship, she nurtures the fantasy of how great life will be with her.

The man I described in the *Manage objections* section said that his former partner used discussions about all the travelling they would do together and all the adventures they would have using her wealth as one of the ways she enticed him to trust that they would have a wonderful, exciting, long partnership. A few months after he gave up his separate life and security, she told him to go away.

7. Service after the sale

In a healthy relationship, this would be the post-commitment phase of give and take. It wouldn't always be easy, but there would be mutual benefits, caring, and consideration. In an abusive relationship—not so much.

This is the phase where Dating Girl disappears and her real personality breaks through. Abuse in a relationship may ramp up slowly or suddenly once the commitment is secured.

An abusive woman may continue to use the manipulation tactics she has learned work on her target while she maneuvered to sell him on the relationship. These selling stages, after all, form a cycle.

After closing the sale, objections may appear that need to be managed, her presentation may need to be repackaged, rapport may need to be reinforced, and the sale may need to be closed repeatedly.

If she tires of the relationship, or thinks the relationship might end, she may start prospecting again for other potential partners.

Chapter 19

Why men stay

"It's unempowering
because people don't recognize what's happening to you,
what you're going through.
You just put your nose to the grindstone and do it."

Why they stay

From the outside, breaking free of an abusive relationship may seem simple. If you're unhappy, just go! But it's not at all simple when it's happening to you.

Some of the reasons men stay in abusive relationships are the same reasons women stay when they are being abused. Some of the reasons are unique to men.

There are many reasons why people choose to stay in abusive relationships, even those that are very abusive.

Some of the reasons men stay are the same as why women stay in abusive relationships. Some of the reasons men hang in there are unique to men.

A man's reasons may be complex and deeply rooted in private and cultural patterns or it may simply be that he knows of no practical alternative. Any of the following may be factors:

- hope that things will get better
- love
- denial
- overemphasis on certain qualities
- guilt
- shame
- fear
- economics
- isolation
- pressure to stay
- lack of support
- physical attraction
- benefits of the relationship
- confusion (brainwashing)
- low self-confidence

Hope

Hope that things can get better is present in most people who stay in relationships that are dysfunctional. When an abused person becomes hopeless that things can get better, that's often the beginning of the end.

Because abuse may come and go in cycles of increasing tension—abuse—decreased tension—back to increasing tension again, the lulls in abuse can keep reigniting hope that the abuse is finished. In the *relief of tension* phase of the cycle, a woman may express regret for abusive behavior or attitudes. She may promise to change. Her remorse and promises may keep hope alive.

There may be hope that the partner will get help and the demeaning, controlling, and/or punishing behavior will go away. There may be hope that whatever outside or internal influences are contributing to her challenging behaviors and attitudes will go away.

People who are the targets of abuse often struggle to figure out what they can do differently so that they can make their partner happy. There is hope that they just haven't found the magic formula yet. They have hope that they will figure it out, they will be good enough or do enough, and everything will be better.

> There are often many false starts at leaving an abusive relationship. It is easy to get pulled back in.

A man may make a decision to end an abusive relationship, but get renewed hope when his partner makes promises of change. Her promises may make it difficult for him to stay on course with the breakup without feeling like he is quitting too easily.

Love

A man may stay with an abusive partner because he loves her despite the abuse. In cases where the abuse is relatively minor or where the abuse is linked to physical illness, it is relatively easy for outsiders to see why he would love her. In cases where abuse is more severe, it may be more difficult to understand his love, but it may still be strong enough to keep up his will to try and make things work.

He may:

- love the personality that periodically returns as she moves through the *relief of tension* portion of the abuse cycle;
- love her non-abusive qualities enough to try to overlook her challenging behaviors and attitudes;
- still be in love with the Dating Girl version of his partner, even though that personality has been superseded by her abusive self; or
- have a distorted view of what love looks like and feels like.

There are many possible reasons why a man might have a distorted view of what love looks like and feels like. He may:

- have been raised by parents who treated him or each other in ways similar to the abusive ways his partner now treats him,
- have had early experiences being the target of abuse by other girls/women,
- be around couples that model abusive behavior, or
- be inexperienced with women.

Denial

People often find it difficult to admit to themselves that they are abused. This is especially true for male targets of abuse, because the idea goes against cultural expectations about men and women and their relationship to each other.

When the culture he lives in largely denies the existence of the abuse of men by women, it only stands to reason that a man may have difficulty wrapping his head around it when it happens to him.

Many elements of male training work against a man recognizing he is being abused, including these man-laws:

- emotions aren't important
- be in control of your situation and environment
- don't talk about personal matters (especially feelings)
- don't ask for help
- don't need help
- be strong
- be a protector
- be responsible
- fix things (fix the toilet, the car, fix problems . . .)
- don't be a "girl" (this is a catch-all for any thoughts, feelings, or behaviors associated with females)

In the 1960s and '70s, Betty Friedan and Gloria Steinem helped blow the lid off of the gender roles that confined and restricted females. Though the rules of what it means to be female may not be totally eradicated, they certainly are exposed and weakened. In many ways, girls and women are able to live their lives as individual persons with a wide range of options of how to be and what to be.

The same is not true for men and boys. Very little has been done to examine the downside of many aspects of male training and to adjust the expectations placed on males.

Therapist and author Terrence Real tried to initiate discussion about the damaging aspects of male training and the death grip it has on males. In *I Don't Want to Talk about It: Overcoming the Legacy of Male Depression*, Real points out that:

- "notions of traditional masculinity view the strong expression of emotion as unmanly, so too they prohibit most expressions of vulnerability,"[1]
- "they [men] are taught to foster 'self-reliance,' eroding their willingness to reach for the healing salve of community,"[2] and
- "many men would rather put themselves at risk than acknowledge distress, either physical or emotional."[3]

Real describes men as being experienced at emotional numbing. Emotions are information. When an individual doesn't take in that information and process it, he is handicapped in his ability to identify what works and doesn't work in his life.

> Boys are taught to discount emotional and physical pain.

College professor and therapist Bret Burkholder describes the way his gender is trained to be: "We're taught to minimize our pain. Boys are taught to suck it up. By the time we're five, we learn how to mask scared, mask sad. We're taught to discount emotional pain and physical pain."

For many men, acknowledging that they are abused by a woman places their masculinity into question. Fear of being seen as unmanly clouds their vision and fosters denial.

Overemphasis on certain qualities

Cultural training of what it means to be a good person may create a distorted idea that there is no limit to how much a person should use qualities like patience, determination, or commitment.

Male training can take this a step further by focusing on particular qualities that may set a man up to not give up on a bad relationship. We train men to be determined, courageous, responsible fixers. Men are supposed to take care of their partners and protect them.

> An abusive woman may use her partner's values to trap him, hold him in the relationship, and keep him doing her will.

While each of these qualities is admirable and an integral part of being a good partner, any of them can be overused and become detrimental. Common sayings like those that describe someone as being "generous to a fault" point out the danger of overdoing a quality.

An abusive woman may use her partner's attachment to positive qualities against him. She may take advantage of his determination, courage, responsibility, compassion, perseverance, forgiveness . . . or of his commitment to marriage as an institution or the well-being of his children.

The following are some examples of how overdoing a quality can set a man up to stay in an abusive relationship too long.

He might be overusing forgiveness if:

- he gives her too many chances to change,
- he accepts apologies that are really fault-reversals (apologies that blame him for her behavior), or

- he pushes himself to "forget" past transgressions and opens himself up for being trampled on again.

He might be overusing responsibility if:

- he rescues a Damsel in Distress,
- he sticks too hard to "I can do it" no matter what the reality of the situation is,
- he beats himself up for not being able to fix something that is unfixable, or
- he marries a woman he doesn't love because she says she's pregnant.

At the same time that an individual may overuse some qualities, he may underuse some other qualities that could potentially create balance. Using more of qualities such as assertiveness, authenticity, equality, and justice might help a situation become healthier or expose fatal flaws in a relationship.

For example, he might be underusing equality and justice if:

- he carries all the financial responsibility of the family because she is pretending to be helpless, or
- he puts her *wants* before his and the family's *needs*.

Each of the qualities I have mentioned is also a skill. The skillful use of each quality lies in figuring out how to use it in a healthy, balanced way given particular circumstances.

Developing relationship skills such as responsibility, patience, and determination helps an individual minimize times when he overuses or underuses each of them. Like all skill development, it's a process of experimentation and learning how to get better and better.

Shame and Guilt

Shame and guilt are emotional brothers. They are from the same family of emotions, but they are subtly different from one another. They can work together and/or independently.

Guilt is generally associated with recognizing that you have done something harmful to yourself or others. Shame goes more to the core of how you see yourself and perceive others to see you. Guilt is "I have done something bad." Shame is "I am bad."

Guilt can morph into shame: "I have done something bad" may lead someone to then think "I am bad."

Shame may be felt in a measure directly related to what was done ("Part of me is bad"), or it can expand to being all-inclusive ("I am all bad").

When these emotions are used in a healthy way, they help keep us on track with our values. They make us stop and examine what we are doing and make adjustments if appropriate. They help stimulate personal reassessment, apologies, change, and making amends.

When these emotions are overreactions, they are stifling. They can stop a person from doing something he really should do or compel a person to do something he shouldn't.

> "The worst guilt is to accept an unearned guilt."
> —Ayn Rand

Guilt and shame may be self-inflicted, partner-inflicted, or rooted in other sources. It may be from recent events or long ago. It may be justified or unjustified.

Recognition that you have done something regrettable creates *self-inflicted guilt and shame*. The level of these emotions may be warranted by the situations that stimulated them or they may be overreactions.

Deciding that a particular relationship can't turn into something healthy and happy (or possibly even safe) may stimulate shame in a man because of feeling like he has given up or has failed. As long as he stays and tries to make it work, he hasn't "failed."

A woman may impose *partner-inflicted guilt and shame* on a man through accusations, blaming, berating, or even through flattery. She may send the messages that he has done bad, sick, stupid, or crazy things; that he is bad, sick, stupid, or crazy; or that he would fit any of those labels if he dared do certain things. She may make him believe that she can't live without him.

A man who is told "I love you so much; if you leave me, I can't survive" may feel guilty for even considering ending the relationship.

The man who is the target of abuse may become accustomed to taking the blame. Abusers may blame their partner for the abuse or virtually everything—leading the target of the abuse to become conditioned to accept blame. In this situation, the guilt his partner imposes on him blinds him to seeing her responsibility and keeps him stuck futilely trying to make the relationship better.

Family, community, social groups, or an individual's religion may intentionally or unintentionally use *group shaming* to exert pressure on individuals so that they stay in relationships even when there is abuse.

Male shame

It may seem unmanly or "wussy" to be the target of abuse by a woman. A man may stay in an abusive relationship to avoid the shame he associates with acknowledging to himself and/ or to others that he is abused by a woman.

A man's acknowledgment that he is being abused by a woman goes against male training that men:

- are in control,
- can fix anything, and
- have all the solutions.

Ending a relationship with an abusive woman goes against male training that:

- men are strong and should "tough it out,"
- a man never gives up, and
- failure is a sign of weakness.

An individual man may be ashamed of what other men have done to women and try to make up for it. This *shame by association* may cause him to take on shame for being a member of a gender that has a history of abusing women.

A manipulative woman may nurture this male shame and capitalize on it. She may take advantage of her partner's desire to be a good man. She may use it to get him to comply with her wishes and whims.

The shame that a man carries for the bad deeds of members of his gender may compel him to stay in a relationship to rehabilitate the reputation of males and prove that not all men are unreliable, callous, or chauvinistic.

Fear

Many men stay in abusive relationships out of fear. The fear may be cultivated by the actions and attitudes of a partner or culture, or by his background and personality. A man may stay because there is something familiar about the abuse and intimidating about moving into unknown territory. Repeated experiences of there being a price to pay when his partner feels challenged, or direct threats of consequences, may instill fear of ending the relationship.

A man may stay in a relationship with a woman because he fears any of the following:

- being alone
- the unknown
- failure
- giving up too soon, making a mistake
- letting her down, making her sad
- that she'll disclose his secrets
- appearing unmanly
- having less time with his children
- losing his children or step-children completely
- the safety of children if they are alone with her
- loss of relationships with her family
- losing his place in society
- stimulating her wrath
- financial repercussions to himself
- financial repercussions to his, her, or their children
- financial repercussions to her
- backlash from friends, family, employer, or religious community
- that she isn't capable of caring for herself
- she will follow through on her threats to harm him, children, family, pets, herself . . .

Economics

A man may worry that if his relationship ends he will not be able to cope with the cost of a separate household, a divorce battle, or future support payments. He may be concerned about the financial impact on himself, children (his, hers, or theirs), and/or even his partner.

In more cases than not, when a living-together relationship ends, it is the man that has to leave the home that he is accustomed to and start over. That can be intimidating.

If his partner makes more money than he does, he may be intimidated by the idea of managing on his own, either because he doubts he can be self-sustaining or he is attached to the lifestyle her income affords him.

If his income is equal to or larger than his partner's, he may worry about how he is going to have his own life while potentially having to continue to support his ex.

A man may worry that if his partner becomes his ex, she may enjoy dragging him into court to rack up legal fees. He may worry that she would be willing to distort his/her/their financial picture in court proceedings and win an untenable support award.

There may also be concern that a malicious partner would undermine his business or job through a campaign of disparagement or sabotage.

His concerns may be based on the stories of other men in similar circumstances, his past experience, recognition of his partner's personality, or outright threats voiced by his partner.

Isolation

Abuse is isolating. The shame of being the target of abuse is isolating. The Don't Talk rule of man-law is isolating. On top of all that, a manipulative woman may work at isolating the target of her abuse.

Some women so capitalize on their man's time that he has no opportunity to nurture relationships with friends and family. He may be so consumed with keeping up with an unreasonable share of the family responsibilities that he has no time or energy left over.

> Abused men are isolated by man-law, shame, lack of opportunity, and severed relationships.

A man in an abusive relationship may feel freakish. He may think this is only happening to him. He may avoid socializing with others in an attempt to hide his partner's behavior. He may be ashamed of her. He may be ashamed that he is in this situation.

The Don't Talk rule doesn't discourage all talk. It prohibits talking about emotions. It censors against opening up to friends and family about personal problems.

Then there is the isolation created through manipulation and distortion. A common abusive tactic is to undermine relationships so that the target of abuse is isolated from his support system. An abusive woman may have spent years disparaging her partner's friends and family, causing rifts between him and those that might help him see reality and break free.

Pressure to stay, lack of support to go

Social or philosophical pressure to stay in an abusive relationship may be exerted by a man's culture, family, job, religion, or other sources. The pressure may be against him ending any committed relationship or it may be against him ending a relationship with this particular woman.

His partner may be mean to him behind closed doors, while she is charming to his family, friends, and co-workers. They may unwittingly send him back into her abusive arms if he talks about wanting to get out. They may counsel him that it must be his fault; he just has to try harder to be nice; he just has to do as she says.

The lack of cultural awareness about the phenomenon of women abusing men heaps another level of abuse on men who are the targets of abuse by their wife or girlfriend. If he does reach out for help, he may be met with disbelief at best and, at worst, accusations that *he* must be abusive himself.

Unlike the resources that have developed for women, there are few for men who are targets of abuse. Most online and print materials about partner abuse give lip service to the possibility that men may be the targets of abuse by women, but don't try very hard to present that scenario in their examples.

If there is domestic violence, police and the courts are generally not male-friendly. Men who are physically abused have a very difficult (if not impossible) time finding a shelter that will take them and their children. Support groups for domestic violence are geared around the concept that men are abusers and women are men's victims.

Relationship benefits

A man may put up with an abusive woman because he is attached to or blinded by the benefits of being with her.

There may be many different benefits of a particular relationship:

- access to sex
- prestige
- having a partner (any partner)
- potential for having children
- her income or position
- being connected to a beautiful woman

I have been surprised at what men will put up with to be with a pretty woman.

A good-looking, physically fit, well-accomplished man turned himself into a pretzel trying to appease his manipulative wife. She obviously spent a lot of time and money on looking good. She was pretty and she was difficult to please. She complained about a long list of his behaviors which many others would see as normal and acceptable.

> when the beauty is a beast

This man didn't have much experience with relationships and he lacked confidence that he was worthy of being with a beautiful woman. It was part of what compelled him to try to meet her many demands and adjust to her many criticisms.

Confusion

Abuse is very confusing. It can drain the abuse target and leave him immobilized. It can throw him into a foggy trance. There may be confusion about what's happening and confusion about what to do about it.

Many factors may contribute to a man having difficulty seeing abuse when he is in the middle of it:

- he may have become acclimatized to it slowly
- he is busy putting one foot in front of another
- he is busy trying to come up with something that will make her happy
- he becomes conditioned to believing he is bad and wrong
- the culture says women don't abuse men
- there is a brainwashing element to abuse
- it's difficult to decipher whether her behaviors and attitudes are warranted
- each abusive behavior and attitude belongs somewhere on the abuse continuum—but where?
- overwhelming feelings may stir him to shut down emotionally

There is a fable about a frog in hot water. If you put a frog into boiling water, he will likely jump out and save himself. If you put a frog into tepid water and gradually turn the heat up, he will likely stay in the water and die. In the same way, the target of abuse may not recognize that the heat is getting turned up because he becomes accustomed to it.

Silence around the topic of abuse of men by women adds to abused men's confusion. The cultural message is, "What is happening to you—can't be happening to you."

Low self-confidence

Abuse undermines a person's sense that they are an OK person and that they can manage on their own. Being berated, criticized, and told in so many ways that you are not good enough often makes a person feel—not good enough, not good enough to:

- manage on his own,
- get another partner, or
- be OK.

Partner abuse also often makes the target feel like he needs to stick around and figure out how to be better, how to improve himself so he can become good enough.

The anxiety that being the target of abuse produces may make a man doubt his ability to cope with life on his own. It's a Catch-22. The anxiety is because of the relationship, but he can't see his way out of the relationship because of the anxiety.

After recuperating from having been married to an abusive woman, a man recognized that his self-esteem had spiraled down as the marriage had worn on. He had been busy putting one foot in front of another, trying to keep up, with no time or energy to reflect on what was happening to him.

The isolation from family and friends removed him from the people who may have given his self-confidence a boost. He described how the absence of cultural recognition of the possibility he was being abused added to his downward spiral: "It's unempowering because people don't recognize what's happening to you, what you're going through. You just put your nose to the grindstone and do it."

How abuse impacts men

"When I was married,
I wondered how was I so inadequate
as to not be able to make her happy?

Now, when I look back on my marriage
and see that I was manipulated, I feel foolish.
How did I not see it?
How did I get myself into this situation?"

> "I didn't know other men were going through what I was going through. It felt like I was the only man in the world this was happening to."

Overview

Male targets of abusive women have a great deal of challenge understanding the situation they find themselves in. We (both men and women) are culturally programmed to not be on the lookout for abusive attitudes and behaviors in women.

Male abuse targets find little support in the media or society. Men tend to be isolated by man-law: be strong, don't talk about personal stuff, don't feel, and don't ask for help. Even if they do seek help, the deck is stacked against them finding someone who understands their situation.

Some of the repercussions men experience from being abused, currently or in the past, are the same as women experience in similar situations. Some repercussions are different than those typically experienced by women.

The impact of partner abuse is conditional upon the type of abuse; the degree, frequency, and amount of abuse; the level of entrapment; and the phase of the relationship the couple is in. The impact of being in an abusive relationship may be multifaceted:

- emotional/psychological
- physical
- sexual
- financial
- legal
- spiritual
- social
- romantic

Emotional/psychological impact

The goals of abusive behavior and attitudes are to demean, control, and punish, so it is not surprising that the target of abuse typically feels demeaned, controlled, and/or punished. Being in a relationship with an abusive person can feel like being with an enemy, a spy who is vigilantly watching for any slip-up on your part so she can capitalize on it.

People who are the targets of abuse have different feelings and reactions:

- when it is just beginning,
- while they are enduring the abuse but not understanding what's happening to them,
- when they awaken to the reality of the situation,
- while they struggle to make things better, and
- as they recover from the aftermath (whether the relationship improves or ends).

All forms and types of abuse have emotional and psychological components, so all forms and types of abuse have an emotional/psychological impact.

For men who are the targets of abuse, the abuse may:

- undermine his self-confidence;
- consume him with trying to figure out how to be good enough, do enough, not upset her, fix the situation, or make the "right" decision to stay or go;
- stimulate him to become hypervigilant and uber-alert, watching for changes in her mood; and/or
- burden him with desire to keep the abuse hidden from others.

Being in an abusive relationship can feel like being in a pressure cooker. Here are just a few of the things a man in an abusive relationship may feel pressured to do:

- please
- take the relationship to the next level
- conform
- reject family and friends
- let go of his own priorities

"I feel like a girl."

Men who are abused by their female partners often take a hit to their masculinity. Being the target of abuse doesn't fit cultural stereotypes of how men are supposed to be. The emasculation a man feels because he is being abused by a woman adds on an extra layer of abuse.

Jan Brown, founder of the Domestic Abuse Helpline for Men and Women, recounted receiving a letter from a woman who said her brother was being abused by his wife:

"His wife would scratch him, throw things at him, point a gun at him, break his eyeglasses, flush his medications down the toilet . . . The sister said in her letter that her brother stitched a cut on his arm himself, with a thread and needle, because his wife had cut him and he didn't want to go to the hospital. Can you imagine being so embarrassed that your wife hits you that you do that?

Men are less likely than women to report abuse because they often worry: 'What will people think if they know I let a woman beat up on me?' and 'I don't want to be laughed at; no one would believe me.'"

Men abused by women often feel some combination of the following (this is by no means a complete list):

- confused, overwhelmed
- rejected
- abandoned
- angry
- discouraged, disillusioned, devastated
- embarrassment, shame, guilt, regret
- responsible
- depressed
- off-balance
- denial
- torn
- unappreciated
- foolish or stupid for not seeing it coming, not being able to change her, not doing something about it sooner, not being able to see a way out . . .
- isolated and alone
- freakish
- apart from other men
- unmanly
- powerless
- fear, worry, nervousness, anxiety, panic, stress
- lowered self-esteem and self-confidence
- post-traumatic stress
- not good enough
- pressured and trapped
- grief and loss
- betrayed
- hopeless (possibly alternating with hopeful)
- on edge waiting for the other shoe to drop
- like they're walking on eggshells
- like they can't do anything (or enough) right

"I keep trying to make sense of the nonsense."

"You want to fix it because they say you're bad and wrong."

"I feel isolated because I couldn't make it stop."

"The betrayal is emotionally violent."

Anxiety

All emotions are information. The information in fear is "danger to myself or others." Anxiety is a heightened state of fear. A man who is the target of abuse by his partner may get the emotional message: "Danger!" The fear may grow into anxiety. The anxiety may grow into panic.

The danger that stimulated anxiety may be physical, emotional, psychological, financial, sexual, legal, or spiritual. If an individual overrides the danger message by trying to ignore it, or if he cannot stop the dangerous situation, anxiety may permeate other parts of his life.

The anxiety created from being the target of partner abuse may show up in situations that are disconnected from his partner. The backlog of fear and anxiety may create overreactions to other situations that stimulate a relatively small amount of fear.

"I went through years of hell in my marriage. There was so much chaos circling around her. My mind was spinning with what can I try next to make her happy.

About seven years into it, I started getting panic attacks. I would get anxious and panicky in traffic and claustrophobic in crowds. I had never had these problems before.

After I separated from my wife, my anxiety suddenly got much better. By the time my divorce was done, my anxiety was gone. I realized I had felt trapped in my marriage. I couldn't let myself recognize it at the time, so it showed up in other situations when I felt even a little trapped.

I felt like I needed my wife to help me manage my anxiety. It turned out she was the cause of it."

Grief and loss

We feel grief every time we have a loss, not just a death. Grief is created when we lose something or someone, when we have to give up on a dream, and when we realize what we thought we had was actually an illusion.

A man in an abusive relationship may feel grief from:

- the loss of his identity;
- isolation from friends and family;
- estrangement from groups, organizations, or activities he previously enjoyed;
- recognition that his relationship is not turning out as he had envisioned;
- the loss of hope each time abusive behavior returns after signs that things would be better; and/or
- the loss of the woman he thought his partner was.

When a relationship ends, a man may grieve losing his:

- companion,
- dreams of a happy life together with that partner,
- time with his children,
- home,
- identity as a partner,
- illusion of having a partner who loved him,
- vision of himself as someone who could solve the problems and make the relationship work,
- relationships with her family,
- friends who side with her,
- usual routines,
- finances, and/or
- belief in the possibility of having a happy long-term relationship with anyone.

Anger and depression

Anger is a secondary emotion. Emotional pain that is not dealt with directly can get turned into anger.

Anger will often explode outward in anything from small explosions of biting sarcasm or irritated tone—to large explosions of rage.

> "I went into a black hole. I had struggled for so many years trying to figure out how to make her happy. How do you deal with someone you loved totally betraying you?"

Anger can also implode. That's depression. Many people say that depression is anger turned inwards.

Any emotional pain that is being built up and not processed can turn into anger or depression. You can see from the long list of painful emotions that a man may feel if he is, or has been, the target of abuse (on page 235) that there is a lot of fodder for anger and depression.

Depression may lead to addictive behaviors, suicidal thoughts, attempts, or even completed suicide. (For help, see Chapter 30, *Resources,* page 335.)

I am *not* saying that the source of a particular man's anger or depression is always, or even usually, caused by the woman in his life. I am saying that a possible side effect of being the target of abuse is anger and/or depression.

Abuse *may* be mutual; each partner may be abusing the other. It may be difficult to discern whether a man's anger and/or depression is a result of being abused by his partner, or is contributing to his partner's abusive behavior and attitudes. It's the "which came first, the chicken or the egg" dilemma.

Addiction and other poor choices

An abused man may be drawn to addictive behavior or other poor choices to deal with depression, numb out, escape pain, or boost his self-esteem. Rebelling against a feeling of being powerless in his life may create a draw to unhealthy behavior that offers a false sense of control.

A person can be addicted to just about anything that creates an inner chemical change, such as a burst of feel-good feelings, numbing out of emotions, or an adrenaline rush. Addictive "substances" may be an attractive distraction from an individual's emotional pain.

There is a wide range of potentially addictive substances and activities an abused man may become attached to:

- food
- work
- drugs and alcohol
- love
- relationships
- sex
- anger
- exercise
- gambling

Reasons for behavior don't excuse behavior. I'm *not* excusing a man reacting to being abused by his partner by acting out in unhealthy ways. I'm pointing out that there may be a connection between her behavior and his. It would be his job to recognize why he's making poor choices and figure out how to deal with his situation in healthier ways.

Physical impact

The physical repercussions of being the target of abuse may be directly related to physical abuse, or they may be connected to the emotional and psychological drain of physical or other abuses creating negative physical consequences.

Physical abuse may result in physical damage:

- cuts
- bruises
- black eyes
- damaged ears, eyes, and nose
- broken teeth
- broken bones
- stab or bullet wounds
- burns
- illness due to poisoning
- damaged organs
- concussions
- death

Abuse of any type may have physical side effects:

- insomnia
- sleepiness
- increased or decreased weight
- reduced energy
- memory challenges
- mental distraction
- inability to concentrate
- stress-related illness
- headaches; neck, shoulder, and/or back pain

Sexual impact

Sexual repercussions of abuse may be a result of sexual abuses or a repercussion of the strain of being the target of other forms of abuse.

A man who was abused by a woman (sexually or otherwise) may find it difficult to trust women enough to engage in sexual relationships in the future.

Alternatively, if a man was sexually abused in a previous relationship and he doesn't work through understanding and processing what happened to him, he may be drawn into other sexually unhealthy relationships. Unhealthy sexual behaviors may become normalized to him. He may erroneously conclude that's just what relationships are like.

Men who experience sexual abuse by a woman often feel particularly demeaned, emasculated, and isolated.

Being in, or having been in, a relationship with an abusive woman may contribute to:

- reduced libido,
- sexual frustration,
- feeling sexually inadequate or unattractive,
- apprehension about sex,
- looking outside the relationship to find sexual fulfillment,
- erectile dysfunction, or
- losing control of his reproductive rights.

I am *not* saying that any of these is *always* traced back to being the partner's fault, just that in cases of abuse, they may be rooted in the abuse.

Trampled reproductive rights

> Women who make men fathers against their will trample on their reproductive rights.

Women who manipulate men into becoming fathers when they don't want to, lie to them about birth control, or deny them access to sterilization are divesting those men of their reproductive rights.

> "My wife knew I didn't want any more children after the first two. She decided to get pregnant anyway and just tell me after the fact. I decided to get a vasectomy so that she couldn't do that to me again.
>
> When I went to the doctor he said that since I was married I had to get written permission from my wife before he would do the surgery. I had to get written permission from my wife! She wouldn't give consent. It took until the third time booking the procedure for her to finally give consent."

> This man was trying to take control of whether he would father more children, but was totally denied that right. His wife had complete control over his reproductive rights.

It seems that in the US and Canada, laws don't mandate a wife's consent for a husband's vasectomy, but many doctors require it as a way to ensure that they won't be sued by a patient's irate wife after the procedure is done.

> A mother of four wrote a lengthy blog entry on the Huffington Post website in January 2013, talking about her thoughts as she "picked up the pen to sign my name and give my permission to my husband's urologist for a vasectomy." She didn't reflect at all on the absurdity of her husband needing her "permission," only on the decision she was making to not have any more children.[1]

Financial impact

Financial fallout from being with an abusive woman may be a direct result of financial abuse or a side effect of other types of abuse. Even a short-term relationship can have long-term financial repercussions.

Financial abuses can leave a man's bank account drained, or his earning ability debilitated, or have him spinning trying to keep up with unreasonable financial obligations.

Financial abuses may have direct financial impacts, such as:

- her overspending on herself making it difficult to impossible for him to make purchases for himself and/or the children;
- creating, and/or leaving him with, overwhelming debt;
- her not allowing him to repay loans made to them by his family;
- ruining his credit;
- her spending or gambling away their savings;
- saddling him with untenable support payments;
- destroying his stuff;
- using her position as his business bookkeeper to extract money into her own pocket;
- forcing him to overspend on divorce lawyers; or
- losing their house, cars, and/or other possessions.

Other forms of partner abuse may wreak financial havoc. A man may lose years of productivity to the struggles of an unhappy relationship and then be further overwhelmed, distracted, and financially drained by the aftermath of ending that relationship.

Other forms of partner abuse may negatively impact a man's ability to earn money if:

- he has to focus so much on her "needs" that it takes unreasonable time and energy away from his job,
- she creates disruptions to his schedule that make him lose work time,
- he can't focus on his career because he's too overwhelmed with carrying a disproportionate amount of family responsibility,
- he hides out to prevent co-workers from witnessing physical wounds she inflicted,
- she discourages schooling or training that would better his position because it would take too much time and attention away from her or make him superior to her in some way,
- she actively attempts to undermine him with customers or employers,
- she creates need for an inordinate number of divorce or custody court hearings that take away from work time,
- she refuses as a co-parent to respect his work schedule and purposefully makes it difficult for him to take care of both fathering and work duties,
- his work is disrupted by having to move because of a breakup, or
- she distracts him with dramatic phone calls or texts when he's at work.

> "The ten years I spent with her
> and overcoming having been with her,
> I missed opportunities.
> I worked two jobs to keep up with her spending.
> I hadn't finished school.
> I don't have any tangible assets."

Legal impact

When your partner is willing to lie and cheat her way through the legal process, it's like the pot of poison at the end of the abuse rainbow. A man who goes into divorce with the idea that they will be able to amicably work through custody and settlement issues may be blindsided by his ex's propensity to fight dirty.

Additionally, the current anti-male climate often results in treatment and rulings that are skewed against men. When a partner or ex-partner abuses you *through* the legal system and you are abused *by* the legal system—abuse is heaped upon abuse.

Many men have had negative experiences when they called the police for protection from their violent female partner. They are often not believed, or, even worse, they are accused of being batterers and are arrested. Many have lost trust in the police and justice systems.

"I *literally* got clocked by my wife. I woke up in the middle of the night to her hitting me with the clock radio.

She went to jail for a few days. The day she was released, I arrived home to her throwing my stuff into the front yard. She was yelling and screaming at me. I called the police. I let the police talk me into leaving with just the things in the yard 'and work things out in court.' That was a big mistake.

Even though I had never been at all abusive or threatening to her, she lied and said she was scared of me so she could get a restraining order against me. That meant I couldn't go back to the house for my tools, or documents, or anything.

People don't realize how much having a restraining order on your record hurts you.

Each time I wanted any of my stuff that was at the house, I had to spend a couple of thousand dollars to have a court hearing. Then she wouldn't honor the ruling and I'd have to have another hearing.

Over and over I had to go through all kinds of extra steps for things because of the restraining order.

It came up when they did a background check for my new job. It came up when I rented an apartment. It came up when I was trying to be approved to spend time at my son's new school.

It was embarrassing. I had to explain that it was unjustified each time it came up and hope that they would believe me.

My wife had worked throughout our whole marriage but quit her job the day after I filed for divorce. I had documents from her employer saying she had quit and the day she quit, but she went into court saying that she couldn't undo resigning and couldn't get another job.

She cried to the judge that she had two children to feed and take care of and their father didn't pay support. We'd only been married for a little over a year and they weren't even my kids, but the judge made me pay her support because he felt sorry for her. The facts didn't matter. They didn't care.

I had to pay more years of support to her than I was married to her. (And it's not like we lived together a long time before we were married. She made sure that she got that marriage certificate fast.)"

Spiritual impact

A man may become estranged from his spiritual community or practices as a direct result of spiritual abuse from his partner or as an indirect result of other abuses.

> "My ex robbed me financially and she robbed me of my faith, my spiritual connection."

The fog of confusion that often torments people who are the target of abuse by a partner may include confusion about previously held spiritual or religious beliefs. The relationship may so cut the target to the core of his being that it creates spiritual disillusionment and a crisis of faith.

"I grew up in a Christian household. Attending church was an important part of my life until my wife told me that other church members were being disrespectful to her and were criticizing me behind my back.

I only realized through the divorce process that my wife made things up, lied, and manipulated. By then I was completely disillusioned with religion and spirituality in general; not just because of feeling rejected and betrayed by the church but also feeling that I was let down by God.

If there was a God, why was this happening to me? Why was she getting away with her lies and manipulations, her torturing of me? How could I be experiencing so much pain at the hands of another if God were real?

I had an accident and nearly died. The experience got me to revisit my spiritual beliefs. I realized that my ex had created the stories about the church people; she had conjured up the betrayal. I was able to open myself up to a church again and work on restoring my faith in God."

Social impact

Social isolation can occur as a direct result of a man's partner purposefully destroying or interfering with his relationships with family, friends, co-workers, and others.

Disconnection from people may also be a result of other forms of partner abuse.

"I lost friends because they were uncomfortable being around my wife. They hated the way she mocked and berated me in front of them. They couldn't find a way to tell me at the time, or maybe they tried to tell me but I couldn't hear them.

The same was true of my family. We spent lots of time with my wife's family. They would come and stay at our house for long periods of time, but my family was excluded. The few times we did spend a holiday with my family, they were made so uncomfortable by her that everyone was on edge."

The emasculation and marginalization that a man who is abused by a woman feels can have a negative social impact on his life. The cultural facade that men don't get abused by women forces men abused by women into the shadows. They often feel isolated and alone, apart from other people, especially from other men.

"It's like coming back from Vietnam. Going through being there was bad enough, but coming back—other people couldn't connect. Your mind is expanded so much. They didn't have the same experience. They couldn't understand your experience. You feel like you're in a blank world where people can't connect with you and you can't connect with them."

Romantic impact

For some men, being in a bad relationship draws them toward a quick replacement. Some get lucky, or have learned from experience what to watch out for, and they find a good match; others don't get so lucky or wise, and find themselves with the same woman, only with a different name.

Some men who have been abused by a partner may lose faith in their ability to choose wisely when it comes to partners, fear getting into another bad situation, or become completely disillusioned with romance. They may swear off women for a while or forever.

Even if a man wants to have another partner, his past relationship may haunt him, making him overreact to the next woman. Previous mistreatment by a woman may set up a man to be hypervigilant with any subsequent partners. He may ruin relationships with healthy women by overreacting to reasonable behavior.

An abusive woman may do everything in her power to make her ex unpartnerable or unmarriageable.

A man recovering from a relationship with a malicious woman who is the mother of his children may find himself in between his ex and his next. He may have figured out that it is futile to try to get his ex to behave in a reasonable, rational way, but his next partner may become very frustrated that he doesn't "make" the ex behave differently.

> "I learned the hard way that anything you say to a partner who you think loves you can later be distorted and thrown against you. That has left a mark. I probably have some trust issues now."

Part Five

What to do about it
—For men who are abused

Part Five

Getting a grip on your situation

"The challenge to overcome the abuse in relationships
is to know truth."

Start here

If you are a man who is abused by a female partner, the #1 thing for you to know is that you are not alone. You are *not* the only man this is happening to.

#2 on the need-to-know list: *Not all* women are controlling, demeaning, or punishing. It's *not* just the way women are.

In order to figure out what to do about the abuse, you need to assess your particular situation. This can be more challenging than it sounds. It is much harder to recognize abuse from within a relationship than from the outside.

What you can and should do about being the target of abuse depends on many factors, including:

- whether you're in the relationship because you want it or just because she wants it,
- how long you've been in the relationship,
- what types of abuse are happening,
- where on the abuse continuum her behaviors and attitudes fall,
- reasons (not excuses) for her behaviors and attitudes,
- your reasons for staying,
- whether there are children involved,
- whether you and/or children are in physical danger,
- the quantity and quality of ways you have already tried to improve the situation,
- her openness to hearing your concerns and her self-motivation to work on improvements,
- whether the abuse is mutual,
- financial considerations, and
- availability of resources and support.

Try to clear your head

The struggle of being in an abusive relationship can be mind-numbing. If you are going to see your situation clearly, recognize your options, and make wise decisions about your future, you need to have a clear mind.

Abusive partners may be motivated to keep you in a fog. The fog may be a sense that your ability to think is suspended, or it may be that your mind is spinning so fast that it is overwhelmed. You may need to work at clearing and re-clearing your mind.

Some steps that may help you de-fog your mind:

- Confide in someone safe (friend, family member, co-worker, counselor . . .).
- Learn and practice some relaxation skills. Taking a couple of deep breaths if you begin to feel overwhelmed, stressed, or anxious can slow down and clear your mind. (See Chapter 30, page 340.)
- Remove yourself from the situation by going for a walk, working out at the gym, taking advantage of opportunities to travel for work . . . Use the time to think about your situation.
- Resist the draw to numb out with drugs, alcohol, sex, gambling . . . Your goal is to be able to think more clearly, not throw yourself into a state that stops your mind from spinning but doesn't allow for clear examination of your situation.
- Imagine yourself stepping back to an observer position, as if you are observing your situation. From this once-removed position you may be able to see more clearly.
- If necessary, consider a period of separation.

Friends and family

You may have been resistant to talking to anyone about your situation because of male training to keep things to yourself, shame, or fear of disparaging your partner. But, having someone to bounce ideas off of may help you check your perception and think through options.

Potential responses to you opening up to friends or family run the gamut from clarifying, helpful, and supportive; to well-meaning but lacking in awareness; to unwilling to talk; to rejecting:

- They noticed the abuse long ago and tried unsuccessfully to talk to you about it or kept quiet about their opinion. If you initiate conversation, they may be able to help you see what they see, and support you coping with the situation and processing your options. (This is what I see happen most often.)
- They are limited by their own life experience and can't identify with what it feels like to be abused. They respond with phrases like: "all relationships have problems," not understanding that it is the accumulative effect of abuse that moves it from normal relationship problems to abuse.
- They don't want to get involved in conversation so they avoid the topic or divert to another topic.
- They reject the concept of you being the target of abuse and push you to be more compliant with her wishes.

You may want to confide in people in small steps, testing the waters with individuals to assess whether they are good candidates for being helpful. This doesn't have to be an all-or-nothing proposition; you can open up in stages.

Assessing your situation

There are a number of areas to cover in assessing your situation. The information will help you determine your best course of action.

Breaking down the problem into topic areas may help you clarify your situation and figure out what to do. Aspects to consider in your assessment include:

1. Length/phase of the relationship
2. The categories and types of abuse
3. The degree of abuse you are dealing with
4. Reasons for her attitudes and behaviors
5. Her willingness/ability to change
6. How you got involved with her
7. Your contribution to the situation
8. Your reasons for staying
9. The cost of being in the relationship
10. Your options

You may want to reassess the situation many times as new experiences give you new data to consider and help you see things more clearly.

Your assessment may be quick and easy, or it may take some time and patience. You may have to repeatedly clear your head as you go through this process. This may not be a once-and-done assessment.

When you are trying to assess your partner and your situation, it's important to look for patterns of behavior and attitudes. For example: Many different behaviors viewed separately may leave you hurt, confused, and wondering why she would do each thing; viewed together, they may show a pattern (e.g., self-centeredness, need to control, or propensity to distort the truth) or expose other connections.

1. Length/phase of the relationship

The length and phase of your relationship with a woman that is being abusive will impact your decisions about what to do next.

- If abuse shows up early in the relationship, it may be best to get out while the gettin's good. Get out before you have children together, entangle your finances, or become more trapped.

> If abuse shows up early in a relationship, get out while the gettin's good. "Run, Forrest, run!"

- If abuse shows up shortly after you've made a commitment to your partner (professed your love to her, started living together, gotten married . . .), that tells you that the non-abusive version of her was likely a Dating Girl illusion.
- If you've been together a long time, and you have endured many instances of abuse and tried many ways to have the situation improve, you may decide that it is time to see the writing on the wall and give up hope for change. (You do get to decide that the last go around the abuse cycle—was the *last* go around the abuse cycle.)
- If you've been together quite a while and there are only a few occasions of abuse, or there are many instances of abuse but you haven't tried many ways to fix the situation, those are scenarios that may offer a lot of hope.
- In other situations, you may not have all that much hope that things can be great, but the length or phase of the relationship weighs heavily on your desire to keep trying for improvements in her attitudes and behaviors or your responses.

2. The categories and types of abuse

Is the abuse:

- verbal,
- financial,
- physical,
- sexual,
- spiritual,
- legal, or
- emotional/psychological?

> Look for patterns.

Does it span many categories?

What specific types of abuse do you know she uses within the categories? (e.g., fault-finding is a type of abuse in the verbal abuse category)

What types of abuse do you suspect she may be using?

What patterns do you notice?

Knowing what categories and types of abuse you are dealing with will affect your course of action moving forward. For example, if she is financially abusing you, then you can work on protecting yourself financially.

This analysis may help you recognize danger areas that you had not previously noticed. For example: If you see a pattern of distorting the truth, then ask yourself if you have taken her word at face value when you shouldn't have (e.g., if she's taking care of the family finances, you may want to check to make sure she is being honest about the finances).

Review Part Two, *Ways women abuse men*, to help you identify the categories of abuse present in your situation.

3. The degree of abuse you are dealing with

Mild abuse is understandably less challenging to deal with and rectify than severe abuse.

The degree of abuse is determined by the abusiveness of individual behaviors and attitudes and the accumulation of abusive behaviors/attitudes. Stabbing you with a knife once is very abusive. Stabbing you with a thousand demeaning comments is also very abusive.

Tips for making this assessment:

> Look for patterns.

- It is easy to get distracted by momentary events, whether those are abusive or loving. Try to step back and see the big picture.
- Remember that abuse may be exhibited in cycles. It is not necessarily constant. To assess the degree of abuse, focus in on the abusive parts of the cycle.
- Look at the various ways she is controlling, demeaning, and/or punishing.
- Look for patterns. For example: If she got pregnant accidentally-on-purpose, and she covers up the fact that she bought five pairs of shoes with family money, and she won't let you see your friends—there's a pattern there. They are very different events, but are all selfishly controlling.

If you think the abuse is mild or moderate, you may be right, or you may be underestimating it. Treat moving forward as an experiment to test your theory. If the abuse is severe, proceed with a great deal of caution.

For help with this assessment, review Chapter 2, *About partner abuse*, and Part Two, *Ways women abuse men.*

4. Reasons for her attitudes and behaviors

Reasons for behavior explain the behavior but they don't excuse it. For example: If you recognize that she is controlling because she has anxiety, that doesn't mean that you should just put up with her being controlling. It does mean that if she is willing to get help with her anxiety, you may want to support her while she works on improving.

Recognizing why she does what she does helps decipher:

- whether the condition is temporary or long-term,
- a direction to go in to improve the situation, and
- how changeable the situation is.

If there is an excuse for abusive behaviors/attitudes, look at patterns:

- Do the abusive ways predate whatever seems to be the excuse of the moment?
- Do they go on after an excuse expires or morph into a different excuse?

For help with this assessment: Part Three, *Why women abuse men.*

Caution: Beware of assuming your partner has the same motivations for doing things as you have. It is natural to think that all people think the way we do. If we are basically honest, considerate, and rational, we tend to think other people are basically honest, considerate, and rational. It is not true. Not everyone thinks the same or has the same motivations. Her reasons for doing what she does may not possess any of those qualities. It is a main reason why the average person has a difficult time understanding what's happening to them in very abusive relationships.

5. Her willingness/ability to change

How does your partner respond to your messages that you don't like her abusive behaviors and attitudes?

Does she:

- shut you down by reacting with anger or tears?
- turn things around by accusing you of wrongdoing?
- try to divert your attention?
- put up a pretense of caring or placate you with promises to change but not demonstrate long-lasting effort to do so?
- rotate through the abuse cycle, returning to abusive ways after a period of remorse or less tension?
- do a sales job on you to remove your objections?
- show openness to hearing your thoughts/feelings?
- genuinely try to change but fall short?
- actually change?

What evidence is there that she is:

- self-motivated to change?
- willing and able to do the work of figuring out how to change?

> You should not work harder at your partner's life than she does.

Can she make changes stick? Anyone can change for an hour, a day . . . a short time. Changes need to be lasting.

Some words of wisdom passed on to me when I was working on my counseling degree: "You should not work harder at your clients' life than your clients do." This advice can be transferred to relationships also. You should not work harder at your partner's life than she does.

6. How you got involved with her

Take a good look at how the relationship began.

Did she:

- trap you?
- manipulate you?
- pressure you?
- move her stuff in without you really making a decision that you wanted to live together?
- say she was pregnant?
- appear to be a Damsel in Distress?
- woo you with Dating Girl then morph into someone else?
- sell you on the relationship?
- slowly turn up the heat?

Did the relationship start out innocently and change later?

What did the transition from nice to abusive look like?

Are you predisposed to getting involved with abusive women? If you are, then you may want to get some help working on uncovering and dealing with the factors/ experiences that set you up to be vulnerable in this way.

For help with this assessment, see Chapter 18, *How men get pulled in.*

7. Your contribution to the situation

Sometimes abuse is mutual. Sometimes both parties are behaving badly. It is important to check yourself to see if you may be contributing to the situation. Are you:

- instigating her abusive behaviors and attitudes?
- reacting to them in an abusive way yourself?

To check whether you are abusive, review Part Two, *Ways women abuse men.*

If you think you are acting abusively, then consider why; review Part Three, *Why women abuse men.*

You'll have to alter the genders in your review and think about whether each gender-flipped item can be applied directly to you as a man, but it will give you food for thought.

Caution: Many men I have talked to have taken on too much of the responsibility for their partners' abusive ways. The men have struggled and struggled trying to be the person their partner seems to want, to find the magic words and ways that will make things better.

Sometimes, fighting is one-sided. Sometimes, one person is argumentative or insisting on fighting and the other person is simply trying to cope with his partner's actions and attitudes. He may not be contributing to her bad behavior, but he may not be able to stop it without entirely removing himself from the relationship.

It is important to take responsibility for your actions and attitudes. It is also important to not take on too much responsibility for hers.

8. Your reasons for staying

Take a hard look at why you are staying.

Is each of your reasons:

- based on sound information and thinking?
- something you want to stick with or work on overcoming?

For help making this assessment, see Chapter 19, *Why men stay*.

Notice if your partner has convinced you to stay by working at getting you to:

- walk away from your basic values, or
- wrap your identity around hers.

Caution: If you are staying because you feel like you have invested *so* much in the relationship and don't want to give all that up, ask yourself if it is better to keep on the path you're on for more years or cut your losses and run.

Some relationships are not doable because the two people simply are not a match for each other. Their values and personalities are not in alignment. Neither party needs to be declared "bad" for not being a match.

If you are staying because you fear her retaliation or the unknown, know that more years will most likely only make you more trapped. Is it better to endure more years of abuse inside the relationship or get out and face whatever she might throw at you because you got out?

You get to decide what you want your future to be. It's not all up to her.

9. The cost of being in the relationship

Consider the impact your relationship has on your, and your children's, well-being. Consider each health category:

- mental
- emotional
- financial
- sexual
- spiritual
- legal
- physical

(If any of these are in imminent danger, take immediate steps to ensure the safety of yourself and your children.)

Review Chapter 20, *How abuse impacts men*.

You may think you are protecting your children by staying in an abusive relationship, but it is important to recognize the abuse's impact on your children. The Mayo Clinic website points to the effect partner abuse has on children (they talk about domestic violence, but this may help you think about the impact of all forms of partner abuse):

"Domestic violence affects children, even if they're just witnesses. If you have children, remember that exposure to domestic violence puts them at risk of developmental problems, psychiatric disorders, problems at school, aggressive behavior and low self-esteem.

You might worry that seeking help could further endanger you and your children, or that it might break up your family. Fathers might fear that abusive partners will try to take their children away from them. However, getting help is the best way to protect your children—and yourself."

> Abusive women want their partner to think that there is only one option: her option.

10. Your options

Bring together the information from the other assessments:

1. Length/phase of the relationship
2. The categories and types of abuse
3. The degree of abuse you are dealing with
4. Reasons for her attitudes and behaviors
5. Her willingness/ability to change
6. How you got involved with her
7. Your contribution to the situation
8. Your reasons for staying
9. The cost of being in the relationship

Assess your desire to continue on the path you're on, see if the path can be improved, or get off of it.

Weigh the costs and benefits of staying in the relationship:

- How changeable is the situation?
- What is the likelihood that she will change?
- What are the risks of continuing the relationship?
- Is it worth the work and/or risks?

What are your options if you stay?

- Is there something more that you want to try changing about yourself (improving ways to cope with her behavior or attitudes; adjusting your attitudes/ actions; getting more clarity . . .)?
- How might you help her change?
- Can the relationship be adjusted in some way?

What are your options if you want to end the relationship?

Notice where you have made any limiting assumptions about your options and check those assumptions. Consult with professionals and trusted people to gather information about your options.

Notice any dichotomous thinking where you're only seeing two options. Check what's on the continuum of possibilities between those two options.

It is important to recognize that not all relationships are salvageable. Just like some homes need to be torn down or abandoned because there is so much wrong with them that trying to rehab them would only be a money and energy drain, and even potentially dangerous, some relationships will drain your resources and still not be liveable.

One man recovering from an abusive relationship suggests other men ask themselves: "Would I knowingly start a relationship with someone I know does these things?" If the answer is "no," it may be a signal to get out.

If you decide to stay in the relationship, then experiment with ways to have the relationship improve. Continue to assess your situation while you experiment with change.

The next sections offer help:

- experimenting with improving the relationship
- looking at communication and reaction changes you might make
- setting and maintaining boundaries
- strengthening yourself
- protecting yourself, your children, and your stuff
- maneuvering through the end of a relationship
- dealing with the aftermath of a breakup

Experimenting with change

Life is an experiment.
We are constantly experimenting
to find out
what works and doesn't work.

Experimenting with improving the relationship

Life is an experiment. We are constantly experimenting to find out what works and doesn't work. If you feel invested in the relationship, you may want to experiment with ways to fix it or cope with it.

The experiment may lead to improvement or confirm that you need to end the relationship.

If you want to experiment with the possibility of change and it is safe for you to talk to her about the situation: at a calm time, try to tactfully tell her your thoughts and feelings about what is going on.

> Avoid the use of the A-word (abuse) when you initiate a conversation about your concerns.

Some tips for working your experiment:

- Have your eyes wide open and your mind as clear as possible.
- Take in the information that indicates who your partner really is (not her potential or Dating Girl).
- Genuinely recognize what works and doesn't work.
- Look for what you can improve and determine your limits (you get to have reasonable limits).
- Consider seeking information from outside sources.
- Don't be afraid to ask for help.
- Consider the experiment results in light of the ten assessment areas listed in the previous chapter.
- Look for clues to determine whether the relationship can be healthy, happy, and prosperous; not great but OK; or needs to be let go.

(For a clearer picture of what a healthy relationship looks like, see Chapter 25, pages 313–314.)

If you go for counseling

Contrary to male training, getting the help of a counselor isn't a wimpy thing to do. It takes courage to ask for help.

If you decide to see a counselor together or on your own, properly vet candidates. Not all counselors recognize that women can abuse men; interview potential counselors on the phone to figure out where they stand. Do some of the interviewing without your partner present.

Seeing a counselor yourself may help you think through your situation, develop coping skills if you want to stay, and strategize if you want to end the relationship. If you go to couples counseling, it may be beneficial to seek a counselor that teaches communication skills as part of the counseling process.

Know that a manipulative woman may agree to go to counseling just so she can check it off your wish list. If she isn't honest with the counselor, she will put in time at appointments but won't get anything out of it.

A manipulative woman may agree to go to couples counseling, or even initiate it, because she assumes the counselor will side with her and push you to comply with her wishes. In those situations, she will cut off the sessions if she doesn't feel supported by the counselor. (And probably tell you to call the counselor to cancel the next appointment.)

If a couples counselor tells your partner that she needs to change the behavior you suspect is abusive, and your partner balks at that advice, that tells you that things are not likely to change. That is information for you to take in when you are assessing the viability of the relationship.

Check your reactions

If you have a tendency to react to your partner with anger, it may be helpful to get a handle on your anger. It is easier to tell if she is creating the abusive atmosphere if you are able to calmly respond to her.

Anger is a secondary emotion. There is some type of emotional pain underneath the anger that isn't getting dealt with directly and is getting turned into anger. Expressing the anger typically makes the other person feel threatened. It doesn't lead to resolution of the underlying issues.

When you feel angry, take a couple of deep breaths so you can clear your head. Ask yourself: what is underneath this anger? You may be feeling rejected, or threatened, or unappreciated . . . Any painful or uncomfortable emotion can be turned into anger.

Being able to label the underlying emotions gives you more concrete information so that you can better understand what is happening to you and more constructively express yourself.

Act.
Don't react.

I am *not* saying that you should just take being abused. Assertiveness is the goal. Learning to check your anger will help you respond with assertiveness rather than aggression.

Assertiveness is being able to say what you have to say with tact. It is expressing your honest thoughts, feelings, problems, opinions, wants, and needs in a respectful way.

For more on anger, emotions, and tact, see Chapter 30, *Resources*, for other self-help products I've created.

Improving communication skills

Sometimes abuse is happening in a relationship because one or both of you are poor communicators. Healthy communication between partners includes:

- saying what you have to say with tact (combination of honesty and respect),
- listening in a way that actually works (you each understand the other's thoughts/feelings and feel heard), and
- using a consultation process to work through conflicts, decisions, and problems (so that each of you feels considered and you come up with creative solutions that suit your family).

I've written quick, easy-to-digest booklets on each of these skills. You and your partner may benefit from using those resources or others to work on building better communication skills.

But—communication skills don't fix everything. If your partner is attached to being controlling, demeaning, or punishing, then learning better communication skills isn't going to improve things. She will just twist the new skills around to her own benefit.

It may be that working on a wider range of relationship skills could be helpful. Having a format for discussing respect, honesty, partnership, and other relationship skills may lead to improvement. I have created materials for helping individuals and couples work on these skills also.

But—that doesn't fix everything either. Your partner may remain attached to behaviors and attitudes that are destructive to you.

Setting boundaries

Boundaries are your limits on what you want and don't want to happen. *Tactfully* expressing your boundaries tests the relationship to see if your wishes can be respected.

Just because you tell her clearly what you want and don't want does not mean that your limits and requests will be honored. An abusive partner may push and manipulate her way through boundaries you attempt to set.

> "Daring to set boundaries is about having the courage to love ourselves, even when we risk disappointing others."
> — Brené Brown

You may want to prepare yourself for ways you anticipate she will react to your limits or requests so you can reiterate your boundary rather than let it be ignored. (If she continually resists your reasonable boundary, then that is information for you about her and your situation.)

If she is attached to what she is doing because it works for her, she will resist your boundaries. She may push your boundaries in a variety of ways:

- in-your-face resistance
- an end-around
- creating the illusion of compliance
- distraction
- guilt infliction: tugging on your heart strings
- flattery
- quiet subversion

To take a look at each method of resisting your boundaries, let's use the example of you setting a boundary about finances. Let's imagine you calmly and assertively tell her you want to know what's going on with the finances. Resistance to that boundary could look like:

In-your-face resistance:

She has a temper tantrum or simply says no.

An end-around:

She switches the attention around on you: "I can't go over the finances because you didn't do _____."

Creating the illusion of compliance:

She shows you some of the finances but withholds other information.

Distraction:

"Sure, we'll do that later. Now I have to _____."

Guilt infliction:

"How am I supposed to have time to do that?" or "You don't trust me!" or crying

Flattery:

"You do so much. Don't you worry about that. I'll take care of it."

Quiet subversion:

She says she'll go over it with you but always has an excuse why she can't do it when you have time.

Strengthening yourself

Being the target of abuse by a partner tends to be draining and debilitating.

Your partner may have kept you so focused on pleasing her that any time and energy for taking care of yourself has been greatly diminished or is non-existent. Your sense of being your own man and your self-confidence may be severely eroded.

> Abusive people don't want their targets to be strong. The more abusive they are, the more they want others to be malleable to their whims.

Remember that her opinion of you or anything else is just her opinion. It may not be how you see things. It may not be right. It may be distorted by her history, health, or motivations.

We are each made up of our biology (genetics and health), everything that's ever happened to us, and everything we've ever been exposed to. That combination creates our thoughts, feelings, wants, needs, problems, and opinions in the moment.

Let her own her thoughts, feelings, wants, needs, problems, and opinions, and you own yours. You can consider hers, but you still get to have yours.

It will take some work to build yourself back up if you have been torn down or worn out.

Reviewing Chapter 19, *Why men stay*, and Chapter 20, *How abuse impacts men*, may give you some ideas where to start to undo the damage that has been done.

Here's an example of how to rebuild yourself based on what you might notice about yourself from reviewing Chapter 19, *Why men stay*. If you have been in denial, think about:

- How has denial hurt you in this situation (or possibly in other situations also)?
- What beliefs set you up for denial?
- Challenge those beliefs.
- Do you want to adjust your beliefs?
- Based on your current life experience, what do you want your related beliefs to be?
- When you lift the sight-obscuring screen of denial, what do you see about your partner, yourself, and your situation?

Here's an example of how to rebuild yourself based on what you might notice about yourself from reviewing Chapter 20, *How abuse impacts men*. If you have turned to addictions to deal with the stress:

- Try to get more exercise, even if it's just getting out for a walk.
- Learn how to deal with emotions directly rather than drown them with addictions.
- Recognize that you are joining her in the abuse: she is destroying you with the abuse and you are destroying you with addictions.
- If you need help, get help.

If you stay in a relationship that is more than mildly abusive, your partner will likely try to undermine your efforts to become strong. You will have to set boundaries and persistently protect them so that you can keep moving in the direction of self-improvement.

Chapter 23

Protecting you and yours

"I didn't listen when I was told to make copies of
documents before I left the house.
I thought it was just a temporary separation
and that I would win her back.
I didn't realize she was already working on
being with the next guy.
I asked and asked to get copies of documents.
She ignored several court orders.
I ended up having to subpoena the records.

If I'd listened when I was told to make copies before I left,
I could have saved myself a lot of
work, anxiety, and expense."

Watch your back

If your abusive partner finds out you are researching about abuse, it may set her off. If the abuse is at the higher levels:

- Don't leave this book lying around.
- Preferably do any Internet research about abuse on devices other than your own. Use friends' devices, or a computer she can't access, such as at a public library or at work.
- Assume she can read your emails and texts.
- Delete your web history on your computer, phone, or tablet. (Wikihow.com/Delete-Web-History may be helpful.)

Get it that a woman is dangerous to you if she has threatened to call the police when you have done nothing to her. Staying in a relationship with such a woman is setting yourself up for being hit with a restraining order. This is a ticking time bomb that could impact your career and life far into the future. (If you skipped over the story of Rob Freeman, Chapter 9, pages 103–105, go back and read it.) At some point, your self-preservation needs to kick in.

You should not be worth more dead than alive. If your partner is very manipulative, controlling, vindictive, or demanding, even if she hasn't yet been violent, it is flirting with death to have a big insurance policy on your head.

Life insurance may be dangerous to your health.

Avoid getting a big life insurance policy if you have any reason for concern. If you've already got one, make an excuse to get rid of it, or change the beneficiary and tell her you've changed it. (Don't make the beneficiary children she could harm or control.)

To protect yourself from financial abuse

Make sure you know the reality of your financial picture:

- If she puts up roadblocks to you seeing financial information, challenge her roadblocks.
- Get documents directly from the originating sources (IRS, banks) if she won't provide them to you.
- Make sure everything you think has your name on it actually has your name on it.
- Examine how retirement and investment accounts and insurance policies are worded. Make sure you are not at risk of losing these in a breakup.
- If you have assets prior to a marriage, make sure you get a strong prenuptial or postnuptial agreement that she can't wiggle out of, and that you are aware of rules about renewing the agreement.
- Recognize that in many jurisdictions she can take everything out of any joint financial accounts.
- If you have any doubts, monitor financial records for her moving money into her own accounts.
- Know your jurisdiction's community property and legal status laws concerning cohabiting couples.

If you have your own business, don't let a partner that you suspect is malicious, self-centered, or manipulative do the bookkeeping. If she's already doing it, check it or insist that it is time for an accountant.

If the relationship is shaky, a manipulative, self-centered woman may press you to give her more control of your personal or business finances as a condition of staying in the relationship. She may want to become more entrenched in your business. Be very careful about letting her in. You may be putting your life's work at risk.

If she lies or manipulates

If you notice that your partner has a pattern of distorting the truth, then it is important to challenge (in your own mind, not necessarily to her) everything that she has ever told you. Stop taking what she says at face value. Ask yourself:

- Is there corroborating evidence to support her story?
- Has anyone ever backed up her story? (Not just regurgitating what she told them.)

For example, she says she was abused by her former partner. Maybe it is entirely true, maybe it is somewhat true, maybe it's an exaggeration, or maybe he was a nice guy who she abused. What's the evidence? Has she kept you away from anyone who could counter her story?

> If you have *any* reason to suspect infidelity, get checked for STDs.

Begin to catch yourself if you recount something as a "fact" just because she said it is so. It may not be true.

If you are skeptical about something she says and want to challenge it, then drill down on it. Challenge those parts that don't make sense to you and see what she says next. A practiced liar will follow up a caught lie with a new lie, evasion, distraction, or some other distortion of truth or avoidance technique. That may be evidence enough that she is lying.

If your partner is a practiced manipulator, then she will create a new way to manipulate you if you stop being manipulated by her old ways. Manipulators are like rivers pushing up against dams. If you plug up one hole, she'll find another vulnerable spot to push through. Be on the lookout for her changeup.

If there is a threat of physical abuse

In every case of physical abuse—there was a first time.

You may be aware that the threat of physical abuse exists because she has been physically abusive in the past, or you may recognize that other forms of abuse can escalate and morph into physical violence. If she tends to go into rages, she may turn on you physically, even if she hasn't so far.

What to do:

1. Make a safety plan. (See the next section.)

2. Respond to physical attacks by trying to keep you and your children safe while not counterattacking.

    *   Know that she may try to provoke you into fighting back so she can get you in trouble.
    *   Leave if possible. (Use your safety plan.)
    *   If you can't get away, dive into a corner and curl up into a ball with your face protected and arms around each side of your head, fingers entwined.

3. Gather evidence.

    *   Get evidence of the abuse and keep it in a safe place (e.g., with family or friends, at work, in a safety deposit box or locker).
    *   Evidence includes: photos; journal of dates, times, witnesses, injuries; medical records; police reports.
    *   If you tell medical staff or police the source of your injuries, you will increase your chances of building a record of the abuse.

Make a safety plan

If there is a chance of physical violence, it is important to make a response plan ahead of time so you can be prepared to keep you and your children safe.

Common advice for safety planning includes:

1. Identify believable excuses for getting out of the house if you see her escalate. Possibly:

    *   walk the dog,
    *   go to the store, or
    *   go out to pick up dinner.

2. Identify the red flags that your partner's anger is ramping up.

3. Identify places in your home and workplace that are relatively safe and dangerous. When an argument is occurring or feels imminent:

    *   avoid spaces with no exit (closets, bathrooms),
    *   avoid rooms with weapons (kitchen, garage), and
    *   stay close to a doorway.

4. Establish a code word, phrase, or sign (a certain light is on or blinking, a shade is down . . .) so that neighbors, family, friends, or co-workers know when you need help. Tell them what they should do if you use the code (call the police . . .).

5. Practice getting out of your home and workplace safely. Notice what windows, doors, stairways, elevators, and other exit pathways work best.

6. Keep your car ready for a fast exit:

   - Keep it well fueled.
   - Park it facing the road.

7. Prepare an emergency stash of personal items and documents for you and the children. (See next page.)

8. Keep track of your phone and keys and try to keep them near you at all times. (But don't count on them.)

9. Hide an extra set of home and car keys and a cell phone. Cell phone options include:

   - a used cell phone that is refurbished to only call emergency numbers, or
   - a prepaid phone that can store phone numbers in case you don't have access to your phone and contact list.

10. Plan where you would go in an emergency.

11. Know the routes to the police, fire station, hospital, and 24-hour stores.

12. If you own guns, know where they are. Assess how to keep them safe and whether it would be best to have them removed from your home. If she uses them against you, you're in trouble; and if you use them against her, you're in trouble.

13. Talk to local domestic violence agencies to determine whether there are resources available to you and your children. (Unfortunately, many don't accommodate men.)

Preparing an emergency stash

Whether or not your partner has ever been violent or ever becomes physically violent, it may be prudent to prepare an emergency stash of important personal items and documents in case she forces you out of your home or you need to flee in an emergency.

Your emergency stash may be hidden in several places or all in one place. You may want some items close by.

Possible storage places include:

- under the spare tire in the car;
- homes of friends, neighbors, family;
- your workplace;
- a rented locker (e.g., at a gym, airport, train station);
- taping keys inside a drawer; and
- in the garage among things she doesn't ever use.

Your emergency stash should include your essential items:

- cash
- credit card
- extra cell phone
- extra keys
- medicine
- eyeglasses
- extra clothes
- copies or originals of important documents (see the *Preparing to leave* section, page 291)
- snacks
- pepper spray
- items for the children
- valuables

Protecting children

An abusive woman may target only her partner or only a specific child or everyone in the household.

Even if your emotionally or physically violent partner only targets you, any children in your home are at emotional/ psychological risk and possibly physical danger as well.

Children may be in physical danger if they are nearby when she physically attacks you. Your safety plan needs to take into account any at-risk children.

Some advice from domestic violence specialists:

- Talk to your children about safety.
- Reassure them that the violence isn't their fault or responsibility.
- Tell them not to get involved if your partner becomes violent with you; explain that it is more important for them to stay safe.
- Scope your home for a relatively safe location they can retreat to.
- Tell them what neighbors or locations they can run to in an emergency.
- Teach them how to call the police or other emergency contacts.
- Create simple code words that indicate that they should leave the house or call for help.
- Practice the family safety plan with them.
- Plan for what you will do if they tell your partner about the plan or if she finds out about it some other way.

Involving police and courts

If you are concerned for your physical safety, or the safety of your children, consider calling the police and/or getting a protection order (restraining order) against your partner.

Realistically, calling the police is a bit of a crap shoot, especially for men. Men who call police for help when they are under physical attack from a female partner have a wide range of experiences. These men are sometimes taken seriously and given assistance, sometimes their situation is trivialized, and sometimes the call for help backfires and ends in the man being arrested himself.[1]

Consider these points about calling the police:

- While police may be helpful to abused men in a relatively small percentage of cases when men call on them for protection, if they aren't called, then there is a 0% chance that they will help.
- When the police do arrive, you undermine their ability to charge or arrest her if you refuse to tell them what happened. You may think that it is chivalrous to protect a woman from being recognized as an aggressor, or feel emasculated by the situation, but should you let those beliefs/attitudes interfere with you getting help?
- If men keep underreporting the incidents of domestic violence against them, it perpetuates the illusion that it isn't happening.
- Reporting the abuse to police helps build a record of her violence. This may be important later.
- There is evidence that there is an increased arrest rate for domestically violent women when there is physical injury, the use of a weapon, or the presence of witnesses.[2]

- A potentially negative outcome from calling the police may be better than being maimed or dead if you don't call.
- If there are children involved, their protection should be paramount.
- There is a chance that calling the police will make her mad and create escalation.

Whether or not police will charge or arrest your violent partner is the first hurdle in legal prosecution. The next hurdle is prosecution itself. A great many domestic violence cases against women are rejected by prosecutors and dismissed by judges.[3]

Another legal avenue to consider is getting a protection order. Protection orders are controversial. There are costs and benefits to trying to get them and having them.

- Like arrests and prosecutions, the odds are stacked against men getting court orders protecting them from their physically abusive female partners.[4]
- Some benefits: Police may be more responsive when there is a protection order in place. She may be less likely to repeat attacks.
- A cost: It may trigger escalation of the abuse.

It is best to find out what your options are in your particular situation and area. Talk the issues through with an attorney, counselor, or male-friendly domestic violence advocate.

If it's over

Abuse is a gift that keeps on giving.

She may call it quits

A very abusive woman, especially a sociopathic one, may call it quits on your relationship when she tires of you, figures she has gotten all she can get out of you from inside the relationship, and/or has found a new target to suck the life out of.

Even if she has been mean, nasty, and horrible to you while you have been patient, forgiving, and kind to her, she will make the demise of the relationship your fault. It couldn't possibly be her fault. She will broadcast accusations of your wrongdoing far and wide.

If you take the bait and grovel to win her back, trying to undo whatever shortcomings she has accused you of, she may use the time to maneuver money and build a relationship with her next target, or just enjoy playing cat and mouse with you.

It may be difficult to accept at the time, but your best-case scenario may be that she finds another man. She may be motivated to not make too many waves so she doesn't expose her true nature to her new "host." He may relieve some of the focus she would otherwise have put on abusing you.

> She may use a divorce as an income-producer, trying to extract as much financial gain for herself as possible.

But, it is not a given that she will go quietly, even if she instigates the breakup and has another guy. Her new man may become her source of funds and support to fight you in court. She may tell him how awful you are, work up his sympathy for her plight, and provoke his manly desire to be her protector.

If you decide to end the relationship

An abusive woman may threaten to leave you hundreds of times and still be mad when you decide to take her up on it. She may want to hang on to her punching bag. If you're gone, who will she look down on so she can feel superior? Who will take care of her? Or serve whatever function you have served in her life?

> A woman who has spent years telling you how much she hates you may react to you ending the relationship with a "How dare you leave me!" attitude.

The answers to these questions, by the way, are *not* your problem. You may be a good deal for her, but she may not be a good deal for you. It only takes one person to decide a relationship has to be over.

Some things to know if you decide to end a relationship with a very abusive woman:

1. It typically takes multiple attempts at ending an abusive relationship before the target of abuse actually gets out.

2. Her initial reaction to you breaking up with her may be to try to woo you back. BEWARE of the WOOING.

3. Abuse often escalates when the relationship ends. Once she realizes you aren't coming back, the wooing may stop and the abuse may become worse than ever.

4. She may skip the wooing-you-back phase and go directly to punishing and threatening you.

To prepare for legal pitfalls, review Chapter 9, *Legal abuse.*

Preparing to leave

If you aren't in imminent danger, you may be able to plan for the end of the relationship. Seek the advice of an attorney if appropriate, so you know your options.

If you are willingly leaving your home, and it appears as if she is working on repairing the relationship, do *not* assume that you will be allowed back in if things turn sour. Get what you need now. If you leave the home without important information or belongings, you may never be able to get back in to get it.

Make sure your cell phone is in your name or that you have control over whether it is disconnected. If she has control over your business or personal phone, she may be able to disconnect it and you could lose your phone number.

Get copies or originals of important documents and stash them in a safe place:

- passport, birth certificate, social security card
- marriage certificate
- bank records for each account
- insurance policies
- your contact list (you might not have your phone)
- medical records
- records of any violence
- lease, mortgage, or title for house and cars
- your partner's social security number, date of birth, and license numbers (car and driver's)
- court orders
- your children's documents, such as immunization records, social security numbers, birth certificates
- tax and business records

BEWARE of the WOOING

When you try to end the relationship with an abusive woman, she may try to win you back. If you are a good deal for her, but she's not a good deal for you, she's not likely to make it easy for you to break free.

If she's trying to woo you back, she may:

- cry,
- get the sad-puppy-dog look,
- tell you she can't live without you,
- become seductive,
- pretend she is the woman of your dreams,
- threaten suicide,
- "attempt" suicide, or
- say she's pregnant.

If you go back to her, chances are high that the abuse will return.

Know that threatening or attempting suicide is *not* a sign of a healthy person. Resist the urge to rescue her or be flattered by the idea that she can't live without you. Direct her towards suicide prevention help; consider contacting her friends, family, or counselor to let them know what's going on; call the police for assistance if you need to; but *don't* try to save her by getting back into a relationship.

If she says she's pregnant, insist on going to a doctor's appointment with her. If she resists the idea, she's probably not pregnant. Even if she really is pregnant, if you weren't happy with the relationship before the child, you're not likely to be happy with it after the child. You may be able to be a better father living separate from the child's mother.

Hold your boundaries

Prepare what you will say/do to hold your boundaries.

You may be the type of person who likes remaining friends with exes but it may not be wise to be friends with an abusive ex. If you try to be friends with her, she may:

- continue to mistreat you like she did during the relationship,
- take you through cycles of nice and nasty,
- capitalize on the opportunity to wiggle her way back into a relationship,
- try to do a sales job on you (see Chapter 18, *How men get pulled in*),
- set you up to zing you, and/or
- use it as cover to manipulate something in the background (e.g., lull you into not preparing well for a divorce while she is maneuvering her advantage).

You need enough time and space to be able to get away from any brainwashing power she has over you.

She may try to manipulate you. Remember to re-clear your head if you go into a fog. Don't act in a fog; buy time to clear your head.

Stop yourself from trying to make everything OK for her. You don't need to fix her sadness, or anger, or disappointment. Let her own it.

Own your own sadness, or anger, or disappointment. Don't react. Acknowledge it for yourself and work through it, but don't impulsively try to make it go away by falling back into old routines.

If you are feeling pressured, have a short statement or phrase that you say to yourself or to her to give yourself time and space to think.

You might say to yourself:

- "I don't need to fix it."
- "Protect yourself."
- "Stand clear."
- "That's her stuff, not mine."

You might say to her:

- "I'm sorry you feel that way."
- "That's your perspective."
- "That doesn't work for me."
- "I'm going to go now" (or "hang up now" or "not respond to your texts anymore")

Do *not* get involved in text wars. If it is difficult to hold your breakup boundaries when she sends you a million angry or pleading texts an hour, then consider blocking her phone number (unless you have to correspond about children). If you are worried that blocking her phone number will make her anger escalate, then resolve not to answer her non-child-related calls and texts.

> Do *not* get involved in text wars.

If you need help resisting her, ask supportive friends and family to help you. Remind yourself about how responding to her has not helped in the past.

Save yourself from a lot of trouble

There is an Arabic saying, "Trust in God, but tie up your camel." Even if you have a hard time imagining your ex would be malicious enough to hurt you financially or physically, it's wise to cover all the bases. (There—I've used religion and a sports analogy in the same paragraph. You pick which works best for you to remember to protect yourself.)

Immediately after a breakup:

- change PINs and passwords to something she wouldn't be able to guess;
- change the locks;
- if there is a garage door opener, change the code of remote controls and keypads;
- watch out for joint bank accounts—she can take it all if she wants to (you might be able to get some back, but you'll have to fight for it);
- if there is physical danger, consider a security system and extra locks; and
- if there is an order of protection against her and/or you, always keep a copy with you.

Stop yourself from seeking revenge or getting even. As Francis Bacon said, "A man who contemplates revenge, keeps his wounds green."

> "A man who contemplates revenge, keeps his wounds green."
> —Francis Bacon

If you need a lawyer, get the best lawyer you can afford. Look for a lawyer who has experience helping men deal with situations similar to yours (e.g., abusive wives in divorce or custody battles).

Prepare for her vengeance

If a woman has lied *to* you during your relationship, she will lie *about* you when it's over. Just know that this will happen, hold your head up high, and gird up your loins.

> "I was on edge, worried at any minute I'd hear that she had turned people against me."

As far as friends and community goes: some people will not be swayed by her, some will believe her for a while and then recognize the absurdity of her accusations, others will permanently join her bandwagon.

It's difficult, but work on not taking it personally. Recognize the pain it causes you, and try to remind yourself that it fits her pattern of distortion of the truth. Let go of some of the people who are pulled in by her lies, and be patient with others.

If she lied and manipulated her way through your relationship, she will lie and manipulate her way through a breakup and divorce. Prepare for a legal battle. She may manipulate her lawyers, the police, judges, and domestic violence advocates.

Some of her lies on court declarations will be constructed to create bunny trails diverting attention away from the actual issues and facts of the case. Your best defense against this is documentation.

Document everything. Minimize voice communication. Keep text messages and emails. Do *not* get pulled into lengthy conversations or arguments. Do *not* write angry emails or text messages to her; they may be taken out of context and used against you.

Children

Once you have a child with a woman, you are connected for life: a painful proposition when that woman is abusive.

Divorcing parents are generally advised to present the idea of divorce to their children in neutral terms, avoiding pointing the finger of blame at one another. That can be very challenging when the basis for the breakup was that their mom was abusive to you:

- It's difficult for her if she is so driven to be absolved of blame that she is compelled to bad-mouth you to the children, even if she has to lie.
- It's difficult for you because you feel mistreated and disparaged by her. It's challenging to watch your children love someone who treated you badly, and find a way to stand up for yourself while not putting your ex down.

When it comes to your children and the relationships with their mother, you will likely often be forced into the position of having to be the bigger person. You will likely sustain many blows to your pride and ego. You may feel betrayed by your children for liking your abuser. You'll have to work through this. Stop yourself from responding to your children's mother with anger.

Your children are half you and half their mom. If you talk badly about their mom in front of them, they may take it personally, as if you are expressing dislike for that part of them that is her. You'll have to weigh that against any potential benefit to them from you enlightening them to the realities of the situation. Any decision to disclose information to the kids should be motivated by gains for them, not for you.

Custody battles

Whether a woman has been abusive because she was irresponsible and dependent or she was in-your-face angry and violent, ending your relationship with her may start a custody battle for your children.

> In the eyes of a court, you can figure that you start in the one-down position as a parent. If your ex is willing to lie, you may move rapidly downwards to lower rankings.

The unfortunate reality is that men are not well positioned to win these battles. Even if she is a terrible mom and you are a great dad, courts may favor her over you in developing parenting plans and custodial rights. They often start with the premise that it is good for kids to be with their mother. It will be difficult to sway them from that position. On the other hand, courts do not tend to be as attached to the importance of kids being with their father.

People can be abusive to their partners and not be abusive to their children, and vice-versa. It is not a given that the woman who is abusive to you is abusive to your children.

A court that is presiding over your custody issues *may* care if your ex has been physically violent against you, but is not likely to care if she has abused you in other ways. They are not likely to care that she has a personality disorder or mental illness unless you show concrete evidence that these directly impact her children in a *very* negative way.

If you feel that your ex is not a good mother and you are arguing to limit her time with the children, your best battle plan is likely to stay solidly focused on how she is with the kids. If she is trying to limit your time/influence with your children and falsely claim that you are a bad father or bad man in general, you will likely have to fight against her accusations.

Your best defense and offense is documentation. Use a dated calendar/journal (electronic or paper) to document everything, including:

- times when you met your parental responsibilities and when she did not meet hers;
- times she made it difficult for you to be with the kids;
- ordinary father caregiving: taking the kids to school, appointments, or activities; making them meals; helping with homework; reading to them; changing diapers . . .;
- any physical violence from her against you or the kids* (see *If there is a threat of physical abuse*, page 281);
- names of the kids' friends, teachers, and doctors;
- any of your ex's activities that get in the way of her being a good parent;
- any incidents when she bad-mouthed you in front of the kids or to the kids; and
- specifics if the kids come back from time with her sick or traumatized.

Never give anyone, or let anyone take, your only copy of a paper journal. Make additional copies if needed.

Use text and email communication instead of verbal. Keep the texts and emails. Don't get pulled into electronic arguments. What you say may be taken out of context and used against you.

*Child protective services should probably be called if you know that one of your children has been physically hurt by your ex while in her custody. If you have an attorney or counselor, they can help you assess the situation.

Recovery

The healing process often can't really start until you are out of the relationship. When you are in it, it's difficult to allow yourself to see how bad it really is. When it's over, you may be overwhelmed with pent-up painful emotions.

Let the realizations and accompanying pain percolate up and acknowledge it. Processing it can help the pain flow through; trying to ignore it can result in it getting stuck inside. (For help processing emotions, see Chapter 30, *Resources*, for other books and materials I've published.)

If she pours on the abuse through a divorce or behaves vengefully after a breakup, it will likely be very painful dealing with her and the havoc she creates.

One man who felt isolated and alone as he went through a nasty divorce from an abusive woman admitted: "I felt like I wouldn't survive the divorce. I went into a black hole. I had struggled for so many years trying to figure out how to make her happy. How do you deal with someone you loved totally betraying you?"

The way to deal with it is to:

- acknowledge the reality of what you have been living with;
- remind yourself that her view of you is distorted by her own agenda, history, and health;
- stop being shocked by her doing what fits her personality and patterns; and
- acknowledge your frustration, regret, feeling foolish and taken advantage of, fear, and other emotions.

In moments of frustration when you are anxious to put everything about her behind you and move on, remind yourself that you need to go through the work of taking care of this first.

A man recovering from an abusive relationship offers this advice: "Whatever she is doing isn't your business. As fast as humanly possible, recognize what's yours and what's not. Put down what's not yours. Lose the anger. Any venom has got to go. The hurt takes longer."

> You need to go through the work of taking care of this first.

If you find your mind going around in circles trying to decipher why she did what she did, and does what she does, take these steps to get back to straight thinking:

- Remind yourself that her reasons may not be rational or logical.
- Stop yourself from assuming she thinks the same way you do.
- Remember that her actions/attitudes fit into patterns. Those patterns may be motivated by selfish desire to control, demean, or punish, not by wanting to be happy, or caring about anyone else.
- Recognize that you no longer need to worry about how you can help her become a better partner to you, or how you can be a better partner to her.

If your ex has sociopathic tendencies—she will try to suck the life out of you like a parasite. It's as if taking away your strength and goodness will strengthen her and make her good. If Martha Stout is right about 4% of the population being sociopathic,[1] lots of us have the misfortune of being paired with sociopaths and dealing with the aftermath of that pairing. Sociopaths don't want you to be happy.

Relief

Quickly or slowly, life should get better.

Even if there is still a mess to clean up, you don't have to live with her anymore. There may be some relief (or lots of relief) immediately upon getting out of a bad relationship or after a divorce is finished, like there was for these men:

"I was never a depressed person before I was married. I was working so hard doing everything, but my wife always found something to criticize. I was always thinking I was the problem. My doctor prescribed an anti-depressant. That helped me cope. After the divorce, I didn't need the medication any more. The depression went away with her."

"It's not a great loss; it's a great riddance."

You can repair relationships with friends and family, like these men did:

"After my wife and I separated, many of my old friends gradually came back, and I was able to rebuild my relationships with my family."

"I didn't realize that my family didn't like my wife. She worked on isolating me from my family first. Then she isolated me from my friends. Once I decided it was over, that's when I found out they *never* liked her. Some of them said they had tried to tell me, but I don't even remember them saying anything. It felt good to get my family and friends back."

Dating again

Sometimes the aftermath of having been in an abusive relationship includes skepticism about relationships in general. It may be difficult to trust another woman when the last one created havoc in your life, drained your energy, or morphed from a friend into an enemy.

Sometimes a man in an abusive relationship meets a woman who gives him a look at what a relationship can actually be. Getting close to a nice woman makes the nastiness of his current partner clearer. The "nice" woman may be a friend who stays a friend or someone who is a new potential partner.

Whether you find a new potential partner before your relationship with an abusive woman ends, or your relationship is over and you are wondering what's next, there are some things to keep in mind so that you can optimize your future.

To protect yourself from getting involved in another abusive relationship, take the time to reflect back on what has happened to you. If you don't learn from your past, history may repeat itself. You may find yourself in a relationship with the same woman with a different name.

> Recognize your kryptonite.

Debrief the abusive relationship experience. Notice:

- what contributed to you being pulled in to the relationship (review Chapter 18, *How men get pulled in*), and
- any red flags that you chose to overlook previously or didn't recognize at the time.

Try to take a new relationship slow. Keep your eyes wide open, taking in the information about who she really is.

To protect yourself:

- Work through any personal issues that may have contributed to you getting pulled in to an abusive relationship.
- Recognize your kryptonite (e.g., Damsels in Distress) and learn to avoid those types of women.
- Don't get so sold on a Dating Girl personality that it blinds you to seeing who she really is.
- Meet her friends and family.
- Look for evidence that corroborates her stories. Don't just take everything she says to be true.
- Pay attention to how she treats other people, not just you.
- Assess all red flags. Pay particular attention to patterns of behaviors and attitudes.
- Act on red flags: either talk to her about them or end the relationship.
- If she is physically abusive: automatic RED FLAG!
- If she seems too good to be true— maybe she isn't true.

> Look for, assess, and act on red flags.

Look for signs the new woman takes responsibility for her attitudes/actions and how they impact other people:

- Does she make a lot of excuses?
- Does she blame others or circumstances for her situation?
- Can she admit to making a mistake?
- Can she give a genuine apology?

Be careful that you don't fall for the opposite of the particular abuse you experienced. Watch out for being attracted to:

- a dependent woman after being with an in-your-face angry woman, or
- an aggressive woman after being with a passive, neglectful one.

Look for a woman who is assertive, rather than either passive or aggressive. Remember that for most qualities, healthy lies somewhere in the middle of the continuum between too little and too much.

Work on developing a healthy balance within yourself so that you attract healthy women and let go of unhealthy ones. Work on learning how to have healthy levels of forgiveness, responsibility, trust, and other relationship qualities/skills.

Trust, like each of the elements found in healthy relationships, is both a quality and a skill. It has its own continuum from too little to too much. It is easy to snap to the *no trust* end of the continuum if you feel burned from having given too much trust to the last woman.

See pages 313–314 for a description of what a healthy relationship looks like.

A healthy level of trust is going to be in the middle of the trust continuum. Look for signs that a woman is deserving of your trust and give it in proportion to her trustworthiness.

(For more on relationship qualities/skills, see *Other publications by Ann Silvers* in Chapter 30, *Resources*.)

Part Six

What to do about it—for everyone

Part Six

For women who are abusing men

"Nobody can go back and start a new beginning,
but anyone can start today and make a new ending."

—Maria Robinson

What women who are abusing can do

The #1 thing for women to know is that it's *not* OK for women to abuse men.

If you think that a particular behavior would be abusive if a man did it to you, then it's abusive if you do it to him. If you have been treating your partner in ways that you would see as abusive if the genders were reversed, then ask yourself why you have thought it was OK for you to treat him that way.

If you are a woman who is being abusive to her male partner now or has been abusive to a partner in the past, then kudos to you for reading this book and trying to figure out how to have healthy relationships.

What to do:

1. Take personal responsibility for your behaviors and attitudes.
2. Listen to your partner.
3. Figure out the what and why of your abusive behaviors and attitudes.
4. Set goals for healthy behaviors and attitudes.
5. Make changes.

Abuse may be mutual. You and your partner may each be abusing each other. You are each responsible for your own behavior and attitudes.

It is important to do a realistic assessment of the part you play in the situation. Recognize if you have a tendency to push the blame onto him when he is reacting to your abusive ways.

1. Take responsibility

It is OK to make a mistake as long as you learn from that mistake.

> Acknowledge yourself for the humility and courage it took to recognize that your behaviors and/or attitudes have room for improvement.

Be patient with yourself as you try to change *and* hold yourself accountable. It takes humility and courage to recognize that you have room for improvement and decide to put in effort to change. Acknowledge yourself for these qualities as you try to change.

What not to do:

- Do not excuse away your behavior and attitudes.
- Do not expect him to "just deal with it."
- Do not blame it on your job, him, your period, or anything else.
- Do not put energy into making positive changes just until he seems to be won back, then slack off and go back to your old abusive routine.

When you notice you have wronged someone, it is important to apologize and make amends.

Apologies need to be genuine. They are not real apologies if they circle around and blame him. "I'm sorry, but you made me do it" is not a genuine apology.

Making amends should ideally be directly related to the wrong done. Giving him a car because you punched him in the face is *not* directly related. The very best way to make amends is to genuinely work on changing the hurtful behavior/attitude.

2. Listen to your partner

Chances are that your partner has been trying to tell you how your behaviors and attitudes have been negatively impacting him, but you have not been receptive to hearing him. He may have long ago given up on being heard.

It's important that you work on being receptive to hearing your partner's thoughts and feelings about your behavior and attitudes.

Many things may have gotten in the way of you really hearing him in the past, including you getting triggered and going into fight or flight. You can't hear people if you get defensive, flee physically or mentally, or go into counterattack mode.

Different scenarios may set off the fight-or-flight response:

- If he expresses himself with anger, you may feel threatened and go into fight or flight.
- Even if he expresses himself gently and tactfully, you may be overly sensitive to criticism and receive it as a threat to your ego.

Just because your partner has a problem with you does not automatically make you bad or wrong. He gets to have his perspective and reaction to the situation and you get to have your thoughts and feelings about it also.

You can listen to him and acknowledge his perspective without agreeing to it. It's important for you to genuinely listen to his side of things and make your own assessment of the validity of his concerns.

3. Figure out what and why

Recognition that you have some behavior and/or attitudes that are harmful to your partner is an important first step in the potential of changing those behaviors and attitudes. You are not likely to change things you think are OK.

Identify the What:

- Review Part Two, *Ways women abuse men*, challenging yourself to identify any of the types of abuse that are a fit for you.
- Try to figure out where on the abuse continuum any of your potentially abusive behaviors/attitudes lie, individually and collectively. Assess each on its own and also assess the collective impact of your patterns of behaviors and attitudes.

Identify the Why:

> Reasons for behavior don't excuse behavior.

- Review Part Three, *Why women abuse men*, for possible reasons why you do what you do and think what you think.
- Remember that there may be more than one contributing factor.
- Remember that reasons for behavior don't excuse behavior.
- Figuring out the reasons helps you understand what the source(s) of the problem is/are and gives direction for making changes.
- Notice if you have been using something as an excuse for your behavior and attitudes. (e.g., "He's angry, so I'm angry back." "I get anxiety if we are running late, so it's OK for me to yell at him about not being on time.")

4. Set goals for healthy behaviors and attitudes

Knowing why you have been behaving in abusive ways in the past helps direct your efforts for change. It gives you some places to start figuring out how to change.

Identifying the ways you have been abusive and why you have been abusive is a good beginning, but it can't end there—you have to change.

To figure out what to do instead of what you've chosen in the past:

- learn what healthy relationship skills look like, and
- get a clear picture of what you expect from yourself.

> Get a clear picture.

Elements of a healthy relationship

In healthy relationships, you each:

- have equal rights;
- have a voice and get heard;
- care what the other thinks and feels;
- support the other to be all they can be;
- work at building healthy relationship skills like respect, compassion, determination, courage, trust, and trustworthiness;
- are able to listen to the other in a way that helps them feel heard and helps you understand what they have going on;
- express your thoughts, feelings, problems, opinions, wants, and needs with tact;
- work towards win-win solutions;

- defer to the opinion of the other in equal amounts (when you can't come to an agreement);
- share responsibility for the household;
- enjoy being around the other;
- participate in decisions about your physical relationship;
- provide a safe environment for each member of the family—physically, psychologically, emotionally, financially, sexually, legally, and spiritually;
- give the other room to have a reasonable amount of separate time for friends, work, and activities;
- try to spend quality time together;
- acknowledge the other;
- accept that it's OK to make a mistake if you work to learn from it and rectify the situation;
- take personal responsibility for your actions (or lack thereof) and attitudes; and
- respect that you each have the individual right to end the relationship.

If your partner is up for continuing to try to have a healthy, happy relationship with you, then you need to be patient as he slowly builds trust in you again. You will have to prove yourself over the long term, not just make short-term changes.

If you genuinely want to change your actions and attitudes, then you will put in the effort for change whether or not your current partner is interested in giving you another chance.

(For more help with relationship skills, communication skills, and emotions, see Chapter 30, *Resources, Other publications by Ann Silvers*.)

5. Make changes

Life is an experiment. As you experiment with change, it is important to be on the lookout for what works and doesn't work.

As you experiment with change, notice when:

> Life is an experiment.

- you reach your goals for healthy actions and attitudes,
- you find it challenging, and
- you don't live up to your standards and values.

Acknowledge yourself for your efforts when you are successful and learn from times you have challenges.

Notice your stumbling points and roadblocks to change. Plan for dealing with the stumbling points in the future and investigate how to address the roadblocks.

Replacing unhealthy relationship skills with healthy ones often happens in a slow progression. You catch yourself earlier and earlier in the performance of undesirable behavior until the healthy behavior becomes automatic.

Behaviors that make it onto the *very-abusive* end of the abuse continuum don't have as much room for error as behaviors that are lower on the scale. If you have been physically abusive, it is too dangerous for everyone concerned for you not to remove the physical abuse from your response repertoire immediately and permanently.

You may need help making changes. If you are open to being helped by a counselor, then seek one who recognizes that women sometimes abuse men.

A woman's story

In Chapter 1, I mentioned a couple who struggled under the weight of the wife's anxiety. She knew she had a lot of anxiety and expected her husband to do whatever she said she needed to minimize her anxiety. She expected him to deal with her irritability and anger that arose out of her anxious feelings.

The anxiety drove her to be demanding and controlling. She rationalized that it wasn't really her that was making the demands; it was the anxiety. If he loved her, he would do what she asked of him.

The man was kind and considerate. He wanted his wife to be happy, but he was worn out with having to live his life in this way. It didn't feel fair or equal. He loved his wife, but he was tired of her irritability.

Eventually, the couple sought help for communication. When the woman really listened to her husband, she realized the harm she was doing to the relationship; she realized that her behavior and expectations of her husband weren't reasonable.

The woman recognized that she had excused away her demands and overreactions. She became motivated to get help dealing with her anxiety. She uncovered the underlying causes of her anxiety and learned how to handle her anxiety in healthy ways.

The woman was surprised by how much better she felt and how much better life was after she broke through her fear of getting professional help. The man was greatly relieved and their relationship was better than it had ever been.

If the relationship ends

Your last chance to change may have been your *last* chance. If he has decided that he wants out of the relationship, you can tactfully express your thoughts and feelings while you also respect his wishes and let him go. It only takes one person to decide to end a relationship. He has that right.

You may not have been a good partner, but you can still choose to be a good ex-partner. You can be respectful and honorable by respecting his wish to end the relationship and handling yourself with integrity during the breakup and after.

You aren't a failure if you learn from your mistakes. You can choose to work on bettering yourself even if your current relationship doesn't survive.

Check your vengefulness. Any satisfaction you get from it will only be fleeting. It will drain your focus and energy. It will make you look bad.

If there are children involved, always keep in mind what is genuinely best for them. It is generally best for them to have a strong relationship with their father.

You can prove yourself as a good mother by:

- assisting in the maintenance of the children's time with their father (unless he is truly dangerous to them),
- presenting the breakup to the children in neutral terms (not assigning fault), and
- not putting down their father to them or in front of them.

For men's family and friends

"My brother's wife was mean and controlling.
I'd get angry sometimes,
wanting my brother to stand up to her.
But we all tried to not cause waves
because he would pay for it."

Impact on family and friends

Partner abuse can be minor to severe, witnessed by family and friends or hidden. People around the target of abuse may experience mildly awkward moments when he is mistreated by his partner, be tormented with worry, or become targets of her abuse themselves.

Sometimes a very abusive woman keeps up a show to the outside world so that even her partner's friends and family don't see what is going on. If he doesn't open up and tell them what's happening behind closed doors, they may not realize he is being abused.

Many times, however, abusive women create turmoil for their partner's family and friends. They bring a poison into his whole circle, spreading destruction like an open vial of Ebola virus brought into the living room.

A woman may start out wooing a new partner's family with her Dating Girl personality, but then show her true self after he is committed to her.

Family and friends of a man being abused by his partner may be:

- blinded by the mask she puts up for the outside world,
- unable to see the abuse or understand it,
- isolated from him,
- trying to figure out how to be helpful, and/or
- trying to appease her so that they can see him, and their nieces, nephews, grandchildren.

They may be confused by:

- how she treats him and them,
- how he responds to her or acts when he is around her,
- his absence,
- why he has turned against them or believes stories she tells about them, and/or
- the control she has over him.

They may feel:

- awkward and uncomfortable;
- abandoned;
- rejected;
- betrayed;
- powerless;
- abused;
- like they have lost their brother, son, grandson, father, or friend;
- frustrated that they are being pushed out and he isn't standing up to her and defending his right to have quality time with them;
- frustrated with him for not getting out of the situation; and/or
- sad.

They may be worried about:

- him,
- his children,
- the ongoing impact on the family,
- her, and/or
- what to do about it.

A sister's story

A sister tells this story of her family's experience:

"My brother's wife was mean and controlling. He did everything to try and please her, to not make her mad. She'd threaten to take the kids and move in with her mother if my brother didn't do whatever she wanted.

She controlled the checkbook. If he wanted something, she'd say there wasn't money. It was frustrating and aggravating to see the kids and his wife in designer clothes while my brother would have clothes with holes in them. He had to beg for work boots.

She was always stirring up trouble in the family. It seems like the whole time they were married, there was turmoil.

We all lived close to each other, but in twenty years, my brother was never allowed to have a single holiday with our family. They spent every holiday with her family. He couldn't even see our mom on Mother's Day.

If she saw me pull into the driveway and the front door was open, I could see her shut the door. She never let me into the house. She'd make sure I felt unwelcome. She wouldn't let my brother go help our mom if she needed help.

She told me the wrong time and place for my niece's graduation, so that I wouldn't be able to be there.

I'd get angry sometimes, wanting my brother to stand up to her. But we all tried to not cause waves because he would pay for it. He has such a big heart. He was torn up when she started hooking up with men online and left him. It took him years to recover."

What family and friends can do

The #1 thing for family and friends of men who are being abused by their partners to know is that it happens: women sometimes abuse men. He is not alone in experiencing it and you are not alone in trying to deal with your loved one being in this position.

This book can educate you about what abuse by women looks like, why she does what she does, how he got pulled in, why he has difficulty seeing what you see, why he is staying, how it affects him, and how you can help.

If you are a close friend or relative, you may want to go through an assessment of his situation to help you figure out your best course of action. Use the advice in Chapter 21, *Getting a grip on your situation*, to assess his situation. You will not likely have all the information, but this still may be helpful to you.

What to do:

- Consider speaking to him about what you see, but recognize that there is a good chance he will defend her or minimize the situation.
- Hang in there. If you keep up as much contact as is allowable, you can be there to help him if he decides he wants your help.
- Be prepared to help him when he is ready. (Review the advice for abused men in Part Five).
- Listen to him when he is ready to talk. You may not be able to fix the situation, but you may be helpful to him by offering a listening ear.
- Remember: it often takes many attempts to leave an abusive relationship before really getting out.

- Try to be patient and understanding of the challenges he faces.
- You may have to work hard at coping with her and appeasing her so that you can protect your relationship with him and his children.
- If you think children are in physical danger, you may need to call your local child protective service.
- Take care of yourself. Consider seeing a counselor who recognizes abuse of men by women.

What not to do:

- Don't confront her. It will probably make things worse for him. She may become angry and make him choose between you and her. This is not likely to go well for anyone.
- Don't demand he choose you or her.
- Try not to be frustrated if he doesn't follow advice you offer; he may not want your advice, just your support.
- Try not to take it personally if he doesn't spend much time with you. He may be trying to appease her.

> You don't get between a man and the woman he sleeps with.

- Try not to take it personally if he accuses you of things you didn't do because she has lied about you. (Do tactfully stand up for yourself, but don't be shocked if he chooses to believe her version of events and not yours. He may eventually see her pattern of lying and wake up to reality.)

I want to acknowledge that you are in a tough position. The cultural blindness to the reality of women abusing men hurts not only the men who are being abused, but everyone who loves and cares about these men.

For all men

"Danger, Will Robinson! Danger!"

—The Robot in *Lost in Space*

The #1 thing for all men to know is that some women abuse some men. It's important to recognize the possibility. This book can serve as a cautionary tale, helping you see what to look out for.

The second most important thing to know is that *not all* women are controlling, demeaning, or punishing. It's *not* just the way women are. Don't accept being abused as if it is expected.

Use the information in this book to:

- learn to pay attention to the red flags of an abusive woman,
- inoculate yourself against the persuasive powers of a Damsel in Distress and the manipulations of a malicious woman,
- help you question male training that doesn't serve you well,
- help you see where a relationship can be headed if she shows early signs of abuse,
- motivate you to get out of abusive relationships early before you become more entangled, and
- educate your sons and daughters about the potential of abuse in relationships.

This book can make you more aware of abusive relationships around you and help you learn how to be supportive of your sons, friends, brothers (biological and figurative), father, and other men who are dealing with an abusive woman. (See Chapter 26, *For men's family and friends*.)

To protect yourself against false accusations of sexual abuse: know that a very malicious woman can conjure up an accusation of sexual abuse with no basis in reality. It's impossible to completely protect yourself from being falsely accused of sexually abusing a woman, but here are some rules to live by to minimize the possibility of false accusations:

- Don't have sex with drunk women.
- Don't have sex with crazy women.
- Beware of having sex while you're drunk or high.

These are tough rules, and not very practical. It's not right or just, but the reality is that current culture sees you as responsible for yourself and responsible for "her" (whoever "her" is). Current culture sees men as bad and women as good, men as liars and women as truth tellers.

> You're still responsible for your actions if you are drunk or high. If she is drunk or high, she's not responsible for her actions—you are.

If she accuses you of sexual abuse while she was drunk, they can say that you were responsible for the sex and pushed it on her.

If she accuses you of sexual abuse, even if she came on to you while you were drunk and you went along with it because you were drunk—she can twist the story and they will probably still see you as responsible and believe that you pushed it on her.

Unfortunately, false accusations of sexual abuse, or any type of abuse, can happen in any relationship phase: acquaintance, first date, casual or committed, even married.

Beware of the signs that a woman has the personality traits to be unstable, overreactionary, delusional, manipulative, punishing, obsessively attached, or a man hater. Recognize that those types of women can be particularly dangerous to you and other men.

Chapter 28

For all women

"The moment we begin to fear the opinions of others
and hesitate to tell the truth that is in us,
and from motives of policy are silent
when we should speak,
the divine floods of light and life
no longer flow into our souls."

—Elizabeth Cady Stanton

The #1 thing for all women to know is that it's *not* OK for women to abuse men. The second most important thing for women to know is that some women are abusing men.

Women need to examine themselves for anti-male, pro-female prejudices.

If you think that a particular behavior would be abusive if a man did it to a woman, then it's abusive if a woman does it to a man. If you think otherwise—why?

Open your eyes to see the evidence around you that we have become a culture that treats men as if they are less than women: less smart, less valuable as parents, less worthy of being treated with respect . . .

Notice how men are represented in the media when they are in relationships with women, how abuse of men by women is treated as expected, funny, and righteous. Stop accepting it. Stop laughing at it. Stop applauding it.

Pay attention to how your friends, mothers, and sisters treat men, and how you treat men. Raise your daughters to treat their partners with respect and expect to be treated with respect. Raise your sons to treat their partners with respect and expect to be treated with respect. Warn them that some men and women are abusive.

Do what you can to bring the reality of the abuse of men by women out of the shadows. Women are, in many ways, in a better position to help with the problem than men are. Men are more likely to be seen as whining about nothing when they try to bring up the topic. Women are more likely to be taken seriously and not be discounted as having ulterior motives. You are in a powerful position to initiate change.

Chapter 29

For helping professionals

"The ultimate tragedy
is not the oppression and cruelty by the bad people
but the silence over that by the good people."

—Martin Luther King, Jr.

Helping professionals can help or hinder

Any man who tries to find help to deal with being abused by his female partner and is met with disbelief, laughter, or disdain is being abused again.

> Any man who tries to find help to deal with being abused by his female partner and is met with disbelief, laughter, or disdain is being abused again.

Helping professionals are not usually in the business of abusing people, but the reality is that many are unwittingly (or purposefully) abusing abused men.

It's way past time for counselors, doctors, police officers, ministers, advocates, and other professionals to recognize that abuse of men by women is happening and be counted as those that are understanding and helpful to the men, women, and children that are impacted.

If you are of the mindset that women abusing men is payback for all the years that the culture turned a blind eye to men abusing women, then you need to be honest with yourself about the vengefulness and faulty thinking of that philosophy.

Do you think that White Americans should have their homes taken away from them or their children forced into culture-annihilating boarding schools because their ancestors abused Native Americans in this way?

If you think that acknowledging the fact that some women abuse some men and that those men are harmed by the abuse somehow discounts the reality that some men abuse some women and those women are harmed by the abuse, then we all need you to question that approach to life.

Do you think that acknowledging pancreatic cancer discounts lung cancer?

Whether or not one happens more often than the other does not change that they both happen, that they are both destructive, and that they both need attention.

We need to work on ways to make life better for everyone, not tit-for-tat punishment or revenge or allowing ourselves to be distracted by fights over relative numbers.

I am *not* advocating that we believe every man that says he is/was abused by a female partner. When you expand beyond the dichotomous thinking that men are bad and women are good, you open yourself to the work of figuring out where the truth lies in each individual situation.

Remember that abusive people sometimes falsely accuse the targets of their abuse of being abusive themselves. Sometimes abuse is mutual. Sometimes there is primary abuse that a partner reacts to with behaviors that belong somewhere on the abuse continuum. It may be challenging to figure out where on the continuum that behavior belongs.

What to do:

- Check yourself for anti-male and/or pro-female prejudices. Do the work to figure out the causes and cures for those prejudices.
- Educate yourself about abuse of men by women. (Reading this book is a great start. Chapter 30 offers further resources.)
- Catch yourself if you discount or minimize abusive acts when they are performed by a woman. A good litmus test is: Would it be considered abuse if the genders were reversed?

- Understand how hard it is for a man to open up and talk about his personal thoughts and feelings, how hard it is for a man to recognize or talk about being the target of abuse.
- Be on the lookout for snippets of information that may be opening the door of disclosure just a crack. Assist that door to open up more.
- Ask questions that get below the surface. For example: If there are children and you suspect the mother may be abusing the father, ask if the pregnancies were planned. Listen and watch for the response to get clues as to whether the pregnancies were conceived "accidentally" on purpose.

Check any literature you disseminate about partner abuse. Does it give lip service to the possibility of men being targets of abuse and then switch to only examples of "he" being abusive and "she" being the target (or even worse—"he" as "perpetrator" and "she" as "victim")?

An abused man who turns to your literature to help him with his situation will have grave difficulty getting insight reading something that bombards him with man = bad.

There is a huge lack of services available to men who are targets of partner abuse and women who are abusive. The void is dangerous to all parties involved: the men who are being abused, their children, and the women who are being abusive. It's important for all helping professionals to figure out how to contribute to filling in this void.

"There are none so blind as those who will not see."
—John Heywood, quoted by Maya Angelou in her last recorded interview

Earl Silverman's plea

Many people have suffered the frustration and desperation that has come with trying to help men who are abused by women. One such advocate, Earl Silverman, could take it no more. In April 2013, Earl ended his misery by ending his life.

Earl had opened the Men's Alternative Safe House (MASH) in his Calgary, Alberta, home three years before his death. It was the only domestic abuse shelter for men in Canada. Earl's home served as a haven for twenty abuse-escaping men and their children before Earl was forced to sell it and close the shelter's doors.

The only funding Earl could find for the shelter's food and expenses was out of his own pocket. When his pocket was empty, he had to give up the shelter and his home.

Earl had fled domestic violence himself twenty years earlier. When he reached out for support at that time, he was treated as an abuser and directed to anger management classes. He felt re-victimized by "helping" professionals.

A friend described Earl and his struggle: "He was a very caring person, very emotional, very direct and honest. He believed very much in fairness and justice and he was just staggered, constantly, that over a period of twenty years that something that is so simple and so logical as gender rights and equality would be so impossible to access for so many people."[1]

Jen Gerson of the *National Post* passed on Earl's plea, "In his note, Mr. Silverman also said he hoped his death would bring more awareness to the issue of male abuse."[2]

Resources

"A bad statistic is harder to kill than a vampire."

—Joel Best,
Stat-Spotting: A Field Guide to Spotting Dubious Data

"Sometimes people hold a core belief that is very strong.
When they are presented with evidence
that works against that belief,
the new evidence cannot be accepted.
It would create a feeling that is
extremely uncomfortable, called cognitive dissonance.
And because it is so important to protect the core belief,
they will rationalize, ignore and even deny
anything that doesn't fit in with the core belief."

—Frantz Fanon, *Black Skin, White Masks*

Internet/phone

For information about deleting web history
wikihow.com/Delete-Web-History

Websites/helplines
(Note: Resources to help abused men are chronically underfunded and therefore understaffed.)

- Amen, UK: amen.ie, 046 9023 718
- ManKind Initiative, UK: mankind.org.uk, 01823 334244
- Domestic Abuse Helpline for Men and Women, US: dahmw.org, 888-7HELPLINE/888-743-5754
- One In Three, Australia: oneinthree.com.au

To investigate mental illness and personality disorders

- Psychcentral.com
- National Alliance on Mental Illness: nami.org
- National Institute of Mental Health: nimh.nih.gov
- Psychopathfree.com
- LightsHouse.org

Suicide prevention

- International hotline information: suicide.org
- US and Canada: SuicidePreventionLifeline.org, 800-273-8255
- Australia: lifeline.org.au, 13 11 14
- UK: samaritans.org, 08457 909090

Articles

Note: Each of these resources is available online. **If you are a man in an abusive relationship, be cautious about leaving evidence of research.** For information about deleting web history take a look at wikihow.com/Delete-Web-History.

Carney, Michelle, Fred Buttell, and Don Dutton. "Women Who Perpetrate Intimate Partner Violence: A Review of the Literature with Recommendations for Treatment." *Aggression and Violent Behavior* 12 (2007): 108–115.

Douglas, Emily, and Denise Hines. "The Helpseeking Experiences of Men Who Sustain Intimate Partner Violence: An Overlooked Population and Implications for Practice." *Journal of Family Violence* 26, no. 6 (2011): 473–485.

Dutton, Donald, and Tonia Nicholls. "The Gender Paradigm in Domestic Violence: Research and Theory." *Aggression and Violent Behavior* 10 (2005): 680–714.

Dutton, Donald, and Katherine White. "Male Victims of Domestic Violence." *New Male Studies: An International Journal* 2, no. 1 (2013): 5–17.

Hines, Denise, and Emily Douglas. "Intimate Terrorism by Women towards Men: Does It Exist?" *Journal of Aggression, Conflict and Peace Research* 2, no. 3 (2010): 36–56.

Kelly, Linda. "Disabusing the Definition of Domestic Abuse: How Women Batter Men and the Role of the Feminist State." *Florida State University Law Review* 30 (2003): 791–855.

Leventhal, John. "Spousal Rights or Spousal Crimes: Where and When Are the Lines to Be Drawn?" *Utah Law Review*, no. 2 (2006): 351–378.

Randle, Anna, and Cynthia Graham. "A Review of the Evidence on the Effects of Intimate Partner Violence on Men." *Psychology of Men & Masculinity* 12, no. 2 (2011): 97–111.

Shernock, Stan, and Brenda Russell. "Gender and Racial/ Ethnic Differences in Criminal Justice Decision Making in Intimate Partner Violence Cases." *Partner Abuse: New Directions in Research, Intervention, and Policy* 3, no. 4 (2012): 501–530.

Additional article resource:

The quarterly journal *Partner Abuse: New Directions in Research, Intervention, and Policy* (Editor-in-Chief: John Hamel) is a valuable resource overall for its gender-inclusive approach to domestic violence. A collection of articles from the journal reports the results of *The Partner Abuse State of Knowledge Project (PASK)*, which is an extensive scholarly review of existing research about partner abuse in the United States, Canada, and the United Kingdom. The five editions of the journal which include the PASK results are available for free online at http://www.ingentaconnect.com/content/ springer/pa.

Books

Anderson, Peter B., and Cindy Struckman-Johnson, eds. *Sexually Aggressive Women: Current Perspectives and Controversies*. New York: Guilford, 1998.

Baker, Amy. *Adult Children of Parental Alienation Syndrome: Breaking the Ties That Bind*. New York: W. W. Norton & Company, 2007.

Baker, Amy, and Paul Fine. *Co-Parenting with a Toxic Ex: What to Do When Your Ex-Spouse Tries to Turn the Kids against You*. Oakland, CA: New Harbinger, 2014.

Cook, Philip. *Abused Men: The Hidden Side of Domestic Violence*. Westport, CT: Praeger, 1997.

Engel, Beverly. *The Emotionally Abusive Relationship: How to Stop Being Abused and How to Stop Abusing*. Hoboken, NJ: John Wiley & Sons, 2002.

Hamel, John. *Gender-Inclusive Treatment of Intimate Partner Abuse: Evidence-Based Approaches*. 2nd ed. New York: Springer, 2014.

Hines, Denise, Kathleen Malley-Morrison, and Leila Dutton. *Family Violence in the United States: Defining, Understanding, and Combating Abuse*. Thousand Oaks, CA: Sage, 2013.

Mason, Paul, and Randi Kreger. *Stop Walking on Eggshells: Taking Your Life Back When Someone You Care about Has Borderline Personality Disorder*. 2nd ed. Oakland, CA: New Harbinger, 2010.

Nathanson, Paul, and Katherine Young. *Spreading Misandry: The Teaching of Contempt for Men in Popular Culture.* Montreal and Kingston: McGill-Queen's University Press, 2001.

Pearson, Patricia. *When She Was Bad: How and Why Women Get Away with Murder.* New York: Penguin, 1997.

Real, Terrence. *I Don't Want to Talk about It: Overcoming the Legacy of Male Depression.* New York: Scribner, 1997.

Sheppard, Roy, and Mary Cleary. *Venus: The Dark Side.* Somerset, England: Centre Publishing, 2008.

Stout, Martha. *The Sociopath Next Door.* New York: Broadway, 2005.

Other publications by Ann Silvers

"a quick look at" full-color booklet series

Demystifying Emotions
Talking With Tact
Listening That Works
Consultation, aka Problem Solving, Decision Making
Anxiety
Partner Abuse
Abuse OF Men BY Women

Booster card set series

Emotional Intelligence Booster
gives you the opportunity to practice the skills of labeling
your emotions and expressing them with tact

Relationship Booster
introduces a relationship Top 40 qualities/skills (tact, respect,
assertiveness, reflection . . .)

Conversation Booster
101 conversation starters with topics ranging from A to S—
amusing to serious and everything in-between

Recordings

The Releasing Waterfall Hypnosis
Anti-Anxiety Hypnosis: Discover Calm
Quit Smoking Hypnosis: Break Free
Diet & Exercise Hypnosis: Get Fit & Stay Fit

Visit silverspublishing.com often for the expanding list of
self-help products.

Chapter 1

1. Kiju Jung et al., "Female Hurricanes Are Deadlier Than Male Hurricanes," *Proceedings of the National Academy of Sciences of the USA*, 111, no. 24 (2014): 8782.

2. Donald Dutton, "The Gender Paradigm and the Architecture of Antiscience," *Partner Abuse: New Directions in Research, Intervention, and Policy* 1, no. 1 (2010): 18.

Chapter 2

1. Peter B. Anderson and Cindy Struckman-Johnson, eds., *Sexually Aggressive Women: Current Perspectives and Controversies* (New York: Guilford, 1998), 9.

Chapter 4

1. Beverly Engel, *The Emotionally Abusive Relationship: How to Stop Being Abused and How to Stop Abusing* (Hoboken, NJ: Wiley, 2002), 28.

2. National Crime Prevention Council, *Stop Cyberbullying Before It Starts*, http://www.ncpc.org/resources/files/pdf/bullying/cyberbullying.pdf.

Chapter 5

1. Anderson and Struckman-Johnson, eds., *Sexually Aggressive Women*, 4.

Chapter 7

1. Connor Kiesel, "Elyria Woman Bites Off Husband's Lip," *NewsNet 5 Cleveland*, March 9, 2012.

2. Albert Biderman, "Communist Attempts to Elicit False Confessions from Air Force Prisoners of War," *Bulletin of the New York Academy of Medicine* 33, no. 9 (1957): 619.

3. "Man Beaten with High-Heel on Waffle House Valentine's Date," *Savannah Morning News*, February 19, 2010.

4. Associated Press, "Jury Convicts Woman in Texas Stiletto Shoe Killing," *The Patriot-News*, Penn Live, April 8, 2014.

5. Antonia Hoyle, "Why are so many MEN becoming victims of domestic violence? It's one of Britain's last remaining taboos, but abuse against men in the home is on the rise," MailOnline, December 4, 2013.

Chapter 9

1. Freeman v. Freeman, 146 Wn. App. 250 (2008).

2. Freeman v. Freeman, No. 82283-2 (WA 2010).

3. Freeman v. Freeman, 146 Wn. App. 250 (2008): ¶6.

4. Ibid., ¶23.

5. Freeman v. Freeman, No. 82283-2 (WA 2010): 1.

6. Freeman v. Freeman, No. 82283-2 (Fairhurst dissenting).

Chapter 10

1. Associated Press, "Texas Woman Pleads Guilty to Sending Ricin to President," *USA Today*, December 11, 2013.

2. Biderman, "Communist Attempts to Elicit False Confessions," 619.

Chapter 15

1. Christiane Northrup, M.D., *The Wisdom of Menopause: Creating Physical and Emotional Health and Healing During the Change* (New York: Bantam, 2001), 46.

Chapter 16

1. American Psychiatric Association, *Diagnostic and Statistical Manual of Mental Disorders*, 5th ed. (DSM-5) (Washington, DC: American Psychiatric Publishing, 2013).

Chapter 17

1. American Psychiatric Association, *Diagnostic and Statistical Manual of Mental Disorders*.

2. Drew Keys, *Narcissists Exposed: 75 Things Narcissists Don't Want You to Know* (Light's House, 2012), 68.

3. Ibid., 69.

4. American Psychiatric Association, *Diagnostic and Statistical Manual of Mental Disorders*, 664, 668.

5. Ibid., 659.

6. Martha Stout, *The Sociopath Next Door* (New York: Broadway, 2005), 6.

Chapter 18

1. Tom Hopkins et al., *Selling All-in-One for Dummies* (Hoboken, NJ: Wiley, 2012), 11.

2. Ibid., 14.

3. Ben DeMeter, "4 Common Sales Techniques People Fall For," Investopedia.com, April 25, 2012.

4. Hopkins et al., *Selling All-in-One for Dummies*, 16.

5. Matt Thomas and Sháá Wasmund, *The Smarta Way to Do Business* (West Sussex, UK: Capstone, 2011), 131.

6. DeMeter, "4 Common Sales Techniques."

Chapter 19

1. Terrence Real, *I Don't Want to Talk about It: Overcoming the Legacy of Male Depression* (New York: Scribner, 1997), 148.

2. Ibid.

3. Ibid., 36.

Chapter 20

1. Allison Tate, "The Change of Life," The Blog, HuffingtonPost.com, January 14, 2013.

Chapter 23

1. Stan Shernock and Brenda Russell, "Gender and Racial/ Ethnic Differences in Criminal Justice Decision Making in Intimate Partner Violence Cases," *Partner Abuse: New Directions in Research, Intervention, and Policy* 3, no. 4 (2012): 507–510; Denise Hines, Kathleen Malley-Morrison, and Leila Dutton, *Family Violence in the United States: Defining, Understanding, and Combating Abuse* (Thousand Oaks, CA: Sage, 2013): 201–204.

2. Shernock and Russell, "Gender and Racial/Ethnic Differences," 509.

3. Ibid., 510, 513–516; Hines, Malley-Morrison, and Dutton, *Family Violence*, 203–204.

4. Shernock and Russell, "Gender and Racial/Ethnic Differences," 510.

Chapter 24

1. Stout, *The Sociopath Next Door*, 6.

Chapter 29

1. Jen Gerson, "Man Who Ran Canada's Only Shelter Dedicated Solely to Male Victims of Domestic Abuse Dies in Apparent Suicide," *National Post*, April 28, 2013.

2. Ibid.

Manufactured by Amazon.ca
Bolton, ON